In 1993, Buffalo County will have been on the map 140 years—as good a reason as any for the directors, officers, and employees of the Waumandee State Bank to decide to underwrite *Buffalo County: A Pictorial History* in appreciation to the community.

In this volume, the heritage of those heroic women and men who first settled Buffalo County is offered as a legacy for all who follow them.

The organizations that are dedicated to preserving that heritage and will benefit from the sale of this book include the Buffalo County Historical Society, which has a genealogy orientation, and the three societies that have museums: Alma (AHS), Mondovi (MAHS), and Fountain City (FCAHS).

BUFFALO COUNTY
A Pictorial History

By Mary Ann Pattison

The photograph on previous spread is of the
Mississippi River at Alma. By and courtesy of Carol Knabe

Endsheet photograph is of the Christopherson farm
on Laehn Bluff in Montana. Courtesy of Eunice Anderson

The photograph on the back of the dustjacket is of the Tundra swans
that rest in Alma every spring and fall. By and courtesy of Jerome Knabe

Copyright © 1993 by Mary Ann Pattison

All rights reserved, including the right to reproduce this work
in any form whatsoever without permission in writing from
the publisher, except for brief passages in connection with a review.
For information, write:

The Donning Company/Publishers
184 Business Park Drive, Suite 106
Virginia Beach, Virginia 23462

Steve Mull, General Manager
Mary Jo Kurten, Editor
L. J. Wiley, Art Director, Designer
Nancy Schneiderheinze, Project Director
Paula Foster, Project Research Coordinator
Elizabeth B. Bobbitt, Production Editor

Library of Congress Cataloging in Publication Data

Pattison, Mary Ann, 1924–
Buffalo County: a pictorial history/by Mary Ann Pattison.
p.   cm.
Includes bibliographical references.
ISBN 0-89865-870-5 (acid-free paper)
1. Buffalo County (Wis.)—History—Pictorial works.   I. Title.
F587.B9P38   1993
977.5'48—dc20   93-4366
                                                   CIP

CONTENTS

Foreword 7

Acknowledgments 9

Chapter 1
From the Beginning 11

Chapter 2
Early Settlers 23

Chapter 3
They Tamed the Land 29

Chapter 4
Building in the County 39

Chapter 5
They Worshiped 51

Chapter 6
Studying and Learning 55

Chapter 7
Business and Industry 61

Chapter 8
Transportation 77

Chapter 9
Cities and Settlements 91

Chapter 10
They Played, They Celebrated 107

Chapter 11
Potpourri 115

Appendix A 124

Appendix B 125

Bibliography 126

About the Author 128

FOREWORD

As we approach the twenty-first century and celebrate 140 years of county history, it is of utmost importance that we remember our past. Since its founding and statehood in 1848, history reminds us of the tremendous role the people here played in the development of Western Wisconsin. It is because of this thought that the Board of Directors of the Waumandee State Bank have agreed to underwrite and present *Buffalo County: A Pictorial History*.

In this volume are preserved the determinations, foresights, hardships and accomplishments of the past generations that have made our county what it is today. This pictorial is a tribute to all that have borne those responsibilities, from original pioneers to today's residents. It is our belief that future generations will continue to provide these virtues of our rich heritage.

The bank would also like to extend its many thanks to those organizations that have made this book possible. Those organizations which will benefit from the sale of this book include the Buffalo County Historical Society, Alma Historical Society, Fountain City Area Historical Society, and Mondovi Historical Society.

The service that is rendered to the community by these organizations is beyond measure. Without them a part of us would be lost. The proceeds of this book will allow each of them to preserve our past and continue to serve the people of our community. It is with this goal in mind that they have published this book.

Let's continue to support them.

Waumandee State Bank Board of Directors

Warren E. Korte   Jacob J. Rosenow   Edward Senty
Lloyd Sendelbach   Paul R. Lorenz

ACKNOWLEDGMENTS

Over one hundred years ago, a comprehensive book called *History of Buffalo County* was written by Lawrence Kessinger. Mr. Kessinger was a teacher, surveyor, county superintendent of schools, historian, "and his handwriting was a thing of beauty." Later historians didn't always agree with him, but Kessinger wrote when many of those early settlers, who knew what had happened, were still around. There will be times when Mr. Kessinger's words (in quotes) were the only way the story could be told. We expect that some will remember events differently than here recorded, and that is fine. Each of us sees or remembers a scene, a picture, or a story in a different light. But, please enjoy the book, and all the memories it could rekindle.

It has been said that a good picture is worth a thousand words. From the over two hundred pictures asked for or offered, a selection had to be made. Hopefully, the pictures and their stories assembled for this book will have captured highlights of the years since humans first crossed Buffalo County. In 1839, a group decided to stay long enough to be called settlers. That was 154 years ago—more years than pages in this book. Not everything could be covered in such a short collection; but if I have one wish, it would be that anyone who has pictures would label them and write down or record their memories. Someday another book could expand what has been written here.

When we accepted the challenge to do this book, we knew there were people who enjoyed sharing their history. The response has been so great that it would be dangerous to try to name all who have helped. Those who loaned pictures are named, but to the many others who told stories, please know that your help made this book possible.

Some personal thanks need to be made. The first meeting with Paul Lorenz of the Waumandee State Bank and with Nancy Schneiderheinze of Donning Publisher's Midwest Division in June, 1992, was the beginning of a very pleasant experience. Frequent calls to Betsy Bobbitt at the Donning Company/Publishers in Virginia Beach, Virginia, kept the book on track. Gene Seyforth of Seyforth Photography was so helpful in making copies of prized pictures. Mary Ann Hurlburt dropped what she was doing many times to help locate things. Virginia Everson read the manuscript and indicated the spots that needed correction. But my greatest thanks go to my husband, Jim Pattison, for encouraging me to go ahead with this book.

These Indians were photographed in the area south of the Tourist Park at Mondovi. They reappeared at times and were friendly with the local people. The photographer, a Mr. Houghton, was in the Mondovi area in the 1890s. Two of the white men are identified as Charles Miller and Art Barrows. A Mrs. Martha Barrows had a millinery shop in Mondovi from 1894 to 1905. Photo courtesy Kristi Schultz

1

FROM THE BEGINNING

Indians, Traders, and Missionaries

Indians were occupants, not settlers of Buffalo County. They had camps where they could grow maize and squash, and where wild fruits and nuts were abundant. The camps lasted as long as fish and game were available for food, and birch for their canoes and tepees remained plentiful. In 1888 Lawrence Kessinger wrote, "Although the Indian has scarcely disappeared from our view...." very little was known about these native inhabitants.

Early French traders were often men of some means and influence, searching for profit and security in the 1680s. Beaver skins were of such importance that they became the "standard of value" for what was bought, sold, or exchanged. Traders were not considered settlers. However, "the necessity of remaining for years at the same post, as well as amorous propensities, soon lead to family relations between the traders and Indians—that is—most traders married Indian women." Lack of education and a tendency to protect their area from competitors meant very little was recorded about the native population.

French missionaries wanted to convert/civilize the Indians. Perhaps their first attempts "were scarcely more than pretensions for opening up commercial resources." The Indian belief/practice of nature gods was in conflict with the idea of civilized people, which tended to make the missionaries intruders. They might have been able to record Indian history, but the Indian had no written language. The French tried to imitate their sounds. For example, Indians did not have a sound for "w," so it was written as "ou" and was a poor substitute in words like Wisconsin—Ouis-con-sin. Going from Indian to French to English disfigured the pronunciation of many names and places.

The area between the Trempealeau and Buffalo rivers was part of a parcel of land that was deeded to the Indians in 1767 and later served as a neutral buffer zone between the warring Chippewa of the north, the Winnebago of the south, and the Sioux across the Mississippi. Traders knew this area was neutral, so they used it for safe travel.

Indians hunted only what they needed. The traders took that limited hunting as a sign of laziness, so they traded brandy for furs. The Jesuit missionaries asked for a ban on the use of brandy, but the Council of Traders told the French king that brandy was the only thing keeping the furs from the English.

The Winnebago Indians refused to fight alongside Black Hawk and got caught in the middle of his war. They were unable to plant their usual crops. Weakened by lack of food and frightened by other Indians, as well as by state and federal troops, tribal leaders signed away their birthright in the treaty of 1825, after being "loaded with rum." They gave up most of their lands in return for an initial thirty-thousand-dollar down payment plus eighteen thousand dollars in cash and three thousand pounds of tobacco each year for the next thirty years. In a treaty signed in 1837, the Winnebago, a broken and starving people, were forced to give up the rest of their land and were moved.

The historic right of the Indian in Buffalo County was taken away by starvation, treaty, false reports of Indian uprisings, and, most likely, by greed.

Northwest Territory

The Northwest Territory was a vast tract of land lying north of the Ohio River, west of Pennsylvania, and east of the Mississippi. It included the states of Ohio, Indiana, Illinois, Michigan, Wisconsin, and part of Minnesota. England took this land from the French after the war of 1763. During the Revolutionary War, violent fighting by the settlers and their Indian allies (1775–1783) helped to win the territory for the United States. Eastern states claimed some of the area but ceded it. Indians signed treaties. As more settlers moved into the region, the territory was divided.

The Northwest Territory, governed by the Ordinance of 1787, was formed into five complete states and a part of Minnesota.

The Path to Wisconsin Becoming a State:

1800–1809	Part of Indiana Territory.
1809–1818	Part of Illinois Territory
1818–1836	Part of Michigan Territory.
1836	Became Wisconsin Territory. Included parts of present-day Minnesota, Iowa, and the Dakotas.
1837	By treaty, the Winnebago and Dakota Indians gave up claim to all land east of the Mississippi River and all islands in that river.
1848	Wisconsin became a state.

Riviere de Beeufs (Beouf)

As early as 1665–1666, buffalo were usually called wild cattle or wild cows by French writers and explorers. Could *Beeufs* have been misinterpreted?

Father Louis Hennepin was sent to explore the upper Mississippi River area in 1680. He would have had little reason to name a tiny river *Riviere de Beeufs* if he had not seen buffalo in the area. But there is some speculation that he had actually ascended the Beef Slough, which at that time was possibly the main channel of the Chippewa River. He said it was full of turtles.

Another story tells that beef cattle tried crossing the river and were mired. It seems that soon after the county was named Buffalo, the Beef River was officially named the Buffalo River. Later maps used Buffalo or Beef river. In 1888 Kessinger wrote, "Newer or more special ones call it Beef River," which was the name in common use locally and at its source in Trempealeau County. Residents don't seem to care what outsiders call it. To them it is still the Beef River. Take your pick.

This aerial photo was taken by Carol Knabe in 1990 of the area now called Beef Slough showing where the Buffalo/Beef River meets the Mississippi. This is the area where seventeenth century explorers said the Bon Secours *and the* Riviere de Beeufs *joined the Mississippi.*

A winter view of the Buffalo/Beef River between Modena and Highway 37 on County KK.

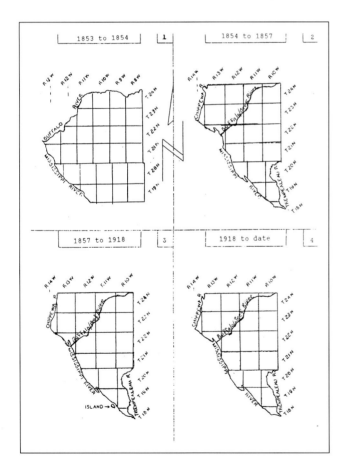

Boundary outlines for Buffalo County. Courtesy W. D. McIntyre Library, Eauclaire Area Research Center

Buffalo were probably gone from the area long before the first settlers arrived. There are reports that buffalo bones were found in the Dover area as recently as 1992.

Buffalo County

Before 1840, present-day Buffalo County was part of Crawford County. In 1850 it became a subdivision of La Crosse County. In 1845 the land west of the Buffalo River and east of the Chippewa River was part of Chippewa County.

Early settlers and speculators thought they still were part of La Crosse County in 1853, but the Pierce brothers had gotten the Wisconsin legislature to make it a part of Jackson County. By an act of the Wisconsin legislature, the boundaries of Buffalo County were established on July 8, 1853. This included land east and south of the Buffalo/Beef River and twelve townships of present Trempealeau County. (See Chart 1)

Judge Gale of Montville (Galesville) saw his sphere of influence slipping away. On January 24, 1854, at his urging, the legislature detached land from Chippewa County and added it to Buffalo County.

Three days later, the legislature detached land east of the Trempealeau River to form that county. A small area west of the Trempealeau River was detached from La Crosse County at the bottom of Buffalo County. (See Chart 2)

In 1857 and 1918 some minor changes were made, but Buffalo County has stayed the same since. (See Charts 3 and 4)

Buffalo County Townships

The topography of Buffalo County consists of two sand prairies, steep bluffs, and narrow valleys dissected by many creeks. One unnamed sage put it this way, "The hills are so steep you could tip over with a three section drag."

The eighteenth, nineteenth, and twentieth townships were surveyed and opened to settlers in 1848. The rest became open in 1853. Between the twentieth and twenty-first townships the lines do not line up. Some maps note it as a *second correction line* used by surveyors to accommodate the curve of the earth.

In 1854 the whole area was called Buffalo, but as the population increased townships were set off. At first any large area could be called a township.

"Fixing up" of towns was a regular concern of the County Board from 1857 to 1881, as areas were adjusted "to afford settlers communication on legal roads."

The following is a list of townships stating when and how they were formed and named, and identifying their first settlers:

Belvidere—April 28, 1855. Belvidere means "a beautiful garden." Kessinger wrote "In 1851 the town of Belvidere, then including the City of Buffalo, seems to have been the most favorable region for settlement." The first school district was established here in 1855. Joseph Berni and John Waecker moved here from Alma in 1850.

Alma—March 13, 1856. W. H. Gates named the village (one version) after reading of a battle on the Alma River during the Crimean War. Christian Wenger and Joseph Richard settled in 1854.

Waumandee—March 13, 1856. This Indian name means "clear and sparkling water." Theodore Meuli and Robert Henry settled on Scotch Prairie (Anchorage) in 1854.

Buffalo (de facto)—March 13, 1856. Used the name of the county. Charles Bipes and Adam Raetz settled in 1851.

Bear Creek—March 10, 1857. Northwest corner that would be changed in a few months.

Naples—March 10, 1857. The name was suggested by Pauline Farrington LeGore for the town where she was born in New York. John LeGore, Henry Adams, and Thomas Hurtley settled in 1855.

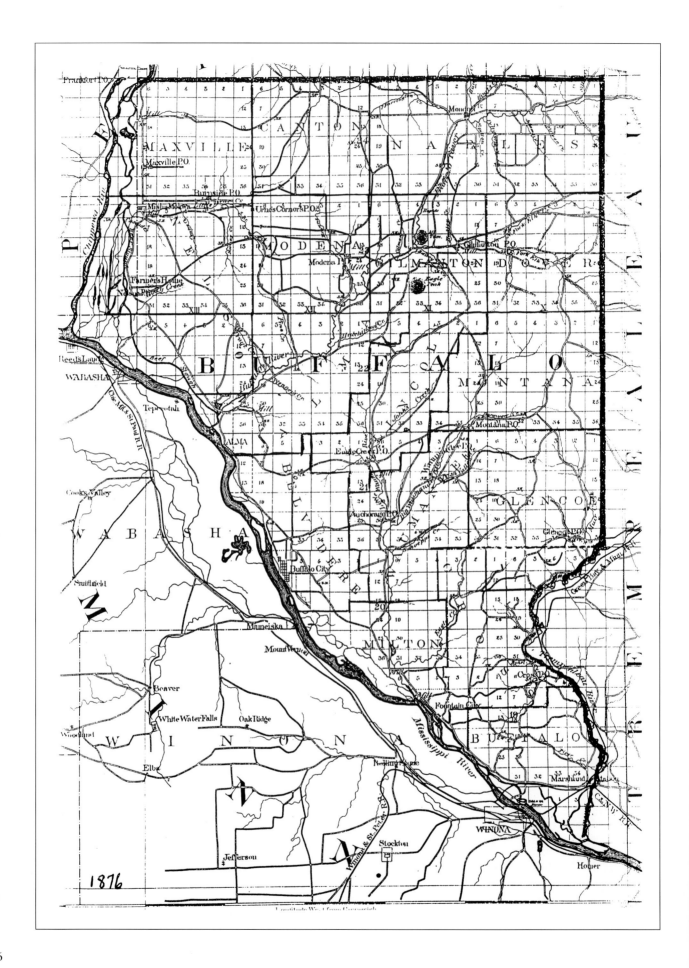

Cold Springs—June 8, 1857. This name was changed to Glencoe at the suggestion of George Cowie for the Valley of Glencoe, Scotland, where his mother was born. Patrick Mulcare settled in 1854.

Cross—November 10, 1857. Kessinger wrote "What made my old friend, Ed Lees, call his town Cross, I never could learn—but perhaps he just felt that way." Peter Schank was the first settler in Cross and also the first farmer in the county in 1850.

Elk Creek—November 10, 1857. Named for the many elk seen in the area. In 1858 it was listed as Gilmantown. The name was changed to Gilmanton in 1897. Daniel Gilman and four sons settled on the west side of the Buffalo/Beef River; Lyman Claflin and Ezra Hutchinson settled on the east side in 1855.

Bloomington—November 10, 1857, (part of Bear Creek). Named for the Prairie that was blooming. Postal officials didn't like the name so they changed it to Maxville. Maxvel and Coleman had arrived with cattle, horses, and household goods that year. William Bean, John Lafferty, Abbott Reed, Michael Aaron, and Rev. Edward Doughty settled in 1855.

Nelson—November 10, 1857, (part of Bear Creek). James Nelson had settled near the mouth of the Chippewa River in the 1840s. W. H. Gates suggested the name to the County Board. Madison Wright was a squatter by 1848 on land his brother later owned.

Milton—November 10, 1857. The name was changed to Eagle Mills in May, 1858, and considered "cheap advertisement of mill on the creek." This mill area caused a drain on the treasury, so the town was vacated and distributed. When Fountain City was set up in 1870, the town of Milton was formed again. Perhaps the name came from the mill. Adam Weber and Michael Obermeier were the first settlers in 1853.

Modena—November 12, 1861. This name was suggested by William Odell and for no known reason. There is a city of Modena in Italy. Orlando Brown broke land in 1856, but didn't move then. William Odell and his sons settled in 1858. The passage of the Homestead Act in 1863 brought Norwegians to the area.

Paige (Page)—Was petitioned as the town of Elizabeth in 1865, but was laid over. It was set off January 21, 1867. At elections in April, "at request of citizens and suggestion of Mr. Glasspool," the name was changed to Canton. The reason is not known. Henry Quackenbos had land in 1855. In 1860 Lewis Kniffin, J. Parr, T. W. Glasspool, Earl Ward, and T. Inschcoe settled.

Montana—July 8, 1867. This name may have been suggested by letters from the Meulis, who moved to the state of Montana during a gold rush.

Montana, in Spanish, means mountainous. Ulrich Von Wald, Christ Kindschy, and August Helwig settled in 1856.

Dover—November 18, 1870. Settlers in the northern part came from Dover, Vermont, and "they thought it altogether fitting to name the new town Dover." Samuel Cooke settled in the lower part in 1855.

Lincoln—November 14, 1871. Charles Jahn suggested the name of the assassinated president. Lawrence Kessinger commented on the irregular shape of the town, "Only those who have seen the country would understand that it was set off that way to aid the town to provide and care for the roads that the people could travel." Henry Mueller and Mathais Profitlich settled in 1853.

Mondovi—(Part of Naples since 1857). November, 1881. Name suggested by E. B. Gifford who read about Mondovi, Italy. Joseph Harvey and Harvey, Lorenzo, Putman, and Harlow Farrington settled in 1855.

Alma Got the Courthouse

The first County Board met March 2, 1854, at the brick home of Henry

Progress had been made on the new courthouse in 1888, so residents had a dedication ceremony. Masons were prominent at the celebration because they were considered "historians in charge of laying cornerstones." The Alma school is in the background. Photo courtesy AHS

County Board members and officers posed for this picture in 1898. Note the fine architecture of the old brick courthouse and the board sidewalk below the steps leading to the second floor. Photo courtesy AHS

Goehrke in Fountain City. This was to be the temporary courthouse, and the officers were to have their offices in their own homes. It was regarded as the de-facto county seat.

As the County Board struggled through its first year, County Judge Marvin Pierce was scheming to have the county seat moved to land the Pierce brothers owned called Sand Prairie. They laid it out, renamed it Upper Fountain City (Merrick Park), and when providence floated stray lumber to the area, they built a "courthouse" for about one hundred dollars. One court session was held in the spring of 1859.

In the Act of Organization of Buffalo County in 1853, a clause stated that the courthouse had to be built on land not subject to "annual inundation" of the Mississippi River. Pierce's land was the only land suitable. In high water, it was an island, otherwise reached only by crossing a swamp.

At a special meeting on July 11, 1859, the question of moving the county seat was voted down. If it hadn't been for the legalism of the Act of Organization, Fountain City may have become the county seat. True, John Buehler and other citizens offered the County Board a new building (Eagle Hotel), "intended and arranged" as the county seat forever. The County board accepted it as far as their authority availed.

About this time, residents of the northern towns demanded that Alma be selected because of its central location. At what would be the last session of the Board in Fountain City, November 15, 1859, the Board exceeded its authority and voted to exclude the recently incorporated city of Buffalo from the Board until the Buffalo City group could poll sixty votes. The legislature passed a law to let all citizens decide if the county seat should be at Alma.

A special election was held in April, 1860. The Board of Canvassers from Fountain City rejected some votes that would have decided for Alma. Eventually, the Supreme Court chose Alma.

In May 1860, the County Board met at the home of F. Richard, where officers were ordered to have their offices until the building of a courthouse. The Cincinnati backers still believed the city of Buffalo had a great future and promised to furnish, free of cost, a suitable courthouse. They even traveled to Alma to possess, figuratively, the offices and papers. They failed. However, the campaign for the county seat compelled the people of Alma to provide as much as Buffalo City had promised. By the summer of 1861, a new courthouse was started.

Kessinger noted that "Animosities raised by the struggle for capital honors had subsided and harmony was again restored." But he could not foresee that a century later (1961) Buffalo County would again be quarreling over whether the new courthouse should be built at Mondovi or Alma.

A last look before this beautiful structure was replaced. The building was constructed of solid brick with stone bands. The first floor basement was used for storage and some offices. Some of the offices on the second floor had ornate fireplaces. The courtroom and judges' chambers were on the third floor. Photo courtesy Sandra Ebert

At first the county jail was in the city of Buffalo. In 1867 it was decided to use part of the 1861 courthouse for the jail. This building was built in 1912 and was torn down when the addition was made to the courthouse in 1988. Photo courtesy Sandra Ebert

The new courthouse (left) was dedicated in 1962. In 1988, offices that had been scattered were all moved into this addition, including Human Services, Extension, meeting rooms, County Historical Society, Sheriff, and the jail. Photo courtesy Sandra Ebert

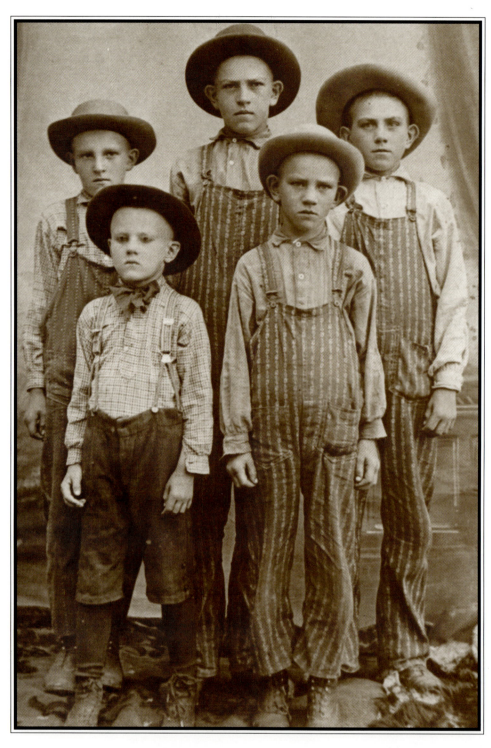

When Mrs. John Bielefeldt went to town to buy material for new overalls for the boys, she had to decide on plain or Indianhead denim. The boys are Henry, Arthur, Helmuth, Alvin, and Rueben. Photo courtesy Hazel Amidon

2

EARLY SETTLERS

Pioneer Men

The first area settler not connected to the fur trade was Rev. Jebediah D. Stevens in 1838. His zeal was to convert the Indians, but when they ignored him, he left for Winona. He may have had contact with Thomas Holmes, who came in 1839.

Thomas Holmes is considered our first real settler because he stayed a few years. Holmes hadn't planned to remain in this area, but ice on the river forced him to stop. In the Holmes party were his wife, Ursula Kennedy, and a foster Indian child, her brother Robert, his wife and two children, and six unnamed helpers. Ursula Holmes was not suited for the wilderness, and there are conflicting stories about her length of stay. Kennedy left about 1846, but whether Ursula left or died is not clear. Holmes then reportedly married an Indian woman. Holmes traded with the Indians, supplied wood to the riverboat people, and "kept a sort of a tavern" at what became Holmes Landing. By 1846 he found the area too crowded, so he headed for Dacotah country. He is credited with founding Shakopee and Chaska, Minnesota, and as many as thirty other towns as far west as Helena, Montana. He ended his days in Alabama with a third younger wife.

Other early settlers at Holmes Landing were John Adam Weber; Henry Goehrke, whose wife is considered the first white woman who stayed; the Andrew Baertsch family; the Nicholas Liesch family; and Christian Wenger.

At Twelve Mile Bluff, three bachelors—Victor Probst, Joseph Berni, and John Waecker—came about 1848.

Madison Wright was a squatter on land across from Wabasha in 1848. Andrew Wright later owned this land but never lived on it.

Overland settlers in northern Buffalo County came later. A group from Dodge County, on their way to Minnesota, heard about land near Augusta.

Thomas Holmes, considered the pioneer settler of the county, was rather an adventurer—who left after the situation ceased to answer his purpose. Photo courtesy FCAHS

Andreas and Mary Berry Baertsch were married in Switzerland and came to America in 1844. In 1847 they came to Holmes Landing, where he chopped wood for steamboats and was part owner of a flatboat. In 1853 he homesteaded in Baertsch Valley in Cross and was welcomed by the first farmer, Peter Schank, already there. Baertsch's son, Anton, was the first white male born in the county Photo courtesy Duane Baertsch

They camped at Bed Bug Station (east of Osseo), where they met a group who spoke about the "land of milk and honey" to be found in the Chippewa Valley. It was decided that Harvey Farrington should go to the Chippewa Valley while the rest checked around Augusta. Harvey went to Eau Claire and on down the river. Near Bear Creek, he met William Van Waters, who described the richness and beauty of Pan Cake Valley (Mondovi). Harvey spent a wild night under the famous Pine Tree surrounded by wolves. In the morning he decided this was the spot to settle and rejoined his three brothers, Orlando Brown, and Joseph Harvey. They returned and established headquarters on June 5, 1855. Abel and Clarissa Farrington came later with Harvey's motherless children. Brown settled in Modena in 1856. Harvey and the Farringtons stayed at Mondovi.

Daniel Gilman and four sons followed the west side of the Beef River and settled in Gilman Valley in August, 1855. Samuel S. Cooke, his wife Lodusky Gardener, five children, and five helpers in a second wagon settled in Dover in 1856.

The Thomas Hurtley family settled in Naples in 1855. Rev. Morse came in 1857 and was the first pastor of the Baptist Church in 1858.

This is an 1891 picture of some of the early settlers in the Mondovi area. Standing, left to right, are Daniel Gilman, Orlando Brown, Joseph D. Harvey, Lorenzo Dow Farrington, and Thomas Hurtley. Seated are Rev. B. F. Morse, Harvey and Putman Farrington. Harlow was the fourth brother. Photo courtesy MAHS

Left: The famous Pine Tree, under which Farrington spent a wild night, keeping a fire going to keep wolves at bay. In spite of pleas to save the tree, the tree was cut down in 1947 to make way for a gas station. This episode was used to call upon local people to organize a historical society to preserve our past. It took a few years for people to think about it. Photo courtesy Mondovi Herald Collection MAHS

Thomas Hurtley and Jane Root were the parents of this family. They had six sons and one daughter. In the back row, left to right, are Bert holding Eva, Henry, Chauncey with infant Charles, Will, and Oliver. In the third row are Josephine (Bert), Ella Wilson, Ione (Chauncey), Isabelle Wilson, Ruby Wilson, Emma (Will), and Jesse (Oliver). Second Row, Mae (Henry) with infant, Jane, Faye, Thomas holding Evelyn, Dema, Harley, and Floy. Front row, Forrest, Harry, Archie, and Hale. Photo courtesy Betty Norby

Funerals were usually attended by everyone in the region. They were solemn affairs with horses driven at a slow walk from the home or church in mild weather and only at a slow trot in cold weather. Hearses could be rented for five dollars. Earl Franzwa drove a hearse like the one pictured here. This unidentified photograph is probably from the early 1900s. Harvey Farrington purchased the site of this home at 574 East Main in 1855. Julian Ede has owned it since 1958. Buffalo Memorial Manor is on the hillside now. Photo courtesy MAHS

We really don't need words to describe this picture, but can we even imagine the feelings these people had after landing here? Maybe things weren't so great where they came from, but here it was a big unknown. How precious that rocking chair must have been. Photo courtesy Murphy Library—Special Collections

Pioneer Women

Chauncey Cooke was sixteen and about to leave with the 25th Wisconsin Volunteers when he wrote this account about a trip his family had made six years before:

My memory takes me back to the 650 miles of journey from the state of Indiana with its daily cares and burdens, especially for my Mother. Yes, the real hardship, as I remember, fell to my Mother. There was the care of brother Kit, a half sick babe nearly always in her arms, during the swaying and jolting of the heavy wagon all day long. Breakfast, dinner and supper brought their manifold tasks of cooking, baking, washing around a smoky fire. The next day and the next, came the same routine for more than six weeks, varied only by storms and sunshine and mud and dust.

Mrs. Cooke's hardships reflect the story of a good many of the pioneer women who settled in Buffalo County. Their first homes are described elsewhere, but their meager homes weren't the only thing that could have discouraged them—loneliness was a big problem. Many left families behind and had new neighbors who often spoke a different language or lived at a distance. The men had to travel to get supplies and were gone for days. In addition to trying to manage a home, pioneer women frequently had to work right along with the men and take over when the men were gone—as many were during the Civil War. As soon as they could, they planted gardens. Wild berries and other fruit helped to fill the food supply. Game was plentiful if the winter allowed the men to successfully hunt. One winter the diet of the Samuel Bond family consisted primarily of bread and wheat coffee.

Clothing was light. Most pioneer children had no underwear until they were grown and could buy their own. They wore hard cowhide shoes but went barefoot as long as weather permitted. The women made the clothes. The same overall pattern was used for man and boy "so the fit was bound to be perfect."

When Fountain City celebrated its centennial, E. F. Ganz (a second generation retired educator, editor, and publisher) spoke of the role of the pioneers:

In spite of the hardships they endured, the pioneers were self-contented, self-reliant, and above all self-supporting. When families did need assistance they did not appeal to authorities but received help from their neighbors.

This is a painting of the special mother at the beginning of this section. Lodusky Gardener Cooke came to Dover in 1855. Photo courtesy Kermit Cooke

Shocking grain was usually a hot job, so the women brought out a lunch and cool drinks. Women often helped shock. In this picture, from left to right, are Vertie, Leslie, and Clayton Amidon, Goldie Kren, Mabel Kent, Ward Kren, and Henry Kent. Photo courtesy Hazel Amidon

Minnie Bade and another lady cutting corn by hand in the Nelson area. Photo courtesy Carolyn Knabe

While men "raised" a barn in Canton in 1917, the neighborhood ladies gathered to help Leopold Fitchenbauer and his mother prepare a meal for the builders. Photo courtesy Fitchenbauer family

Buffalo County has long been a leader in soil conservation. Contour strips like this are common all over the county.

3

THEY TAMED THE LAND

Getting Started

The first survey of land in Buffalo County was done in 1848, and land below Township 21 was opened for pre-emption or sale. The rest of the county was surveyed and opened in 1853.

The first farmer in the county was Peter Schank in the town of Cross in 1850, eleven years after Holmes came. A farmer was considered well off if he owned a wagon, a plow, a yoke of oxen, the most necessary household articles, and an ax. Just a few more tools—for example, a couple of planes, augers, a square, and a hatchet—made him a carpenter or mechanic who took rank with a blacksmith.

The first things settlers looked for were water, wood, and wild hay for their animals. They tended to settle in an area similar to that from which they came. The Swiss and Germans liked the steep river bluffs; English-Americans preferred the bottoms; Norwegians settled farther up the valleys. A few came by wagon, but many walked to their new homesteads.

Settlers had to go to Mineral Point to register their land until an office opened in La Crosse on July 28, 1852. Land was obtained in various ways:

Pre-emption—Squatters moved to a place they did not own, built shelter, but did not get title to the land. Real estate speculators, called "claim-jumpers," often worked with lawyers to get title and take the land from the

The entrance to Camp Gilmanton, the CCC camp, around 1933. During the Great Depression, President Roosevelt established the Civilian Conservation Corps to provide jobs and training for young men. Many projects were undertaken, but the most obvious were the pine tree plantings, earthen dam building, and the contour strips on many farms. The Nelson camp mixed grasshopper bait. Photo courtesy Velva Molland

THE UNITED STATES OF AMERICA,

To all to whom these presents shall come, Greeting:

Homestead Certificate No. 581
APPLICATION 887

Whereas, there has been deposited in the General Land Office of the United States, a CERTIFICATE of the REGISTER OF THE LAND OFFICE at La Crosse Wisconsin, whereby it appears that pursuant to the Act of Congress approved 20th May, 1862, "To secure Homesteads to actual Settlers on the public domain," and the acts supplemental thereto the claim of Thomas W. Glasspoole has been established and duly consummated in conformity to law, for the East half of the North West quarter of Section twenty eight in Township twenty-four North of Range twelve West, in the District of lands subject to sale at La Crosse Wisconsin, containing eighty acres,

according to the Official Plat of the survey of the said Land returned to the GENERAL LAND OFFICE by the SURVEYOR GENERAL:

Now know ye, That there is therefore granted by the UNITED STATES unto the said Thomas W. Glasspoole the tract of Land above described: To Have and to Hold the said tract of Land, with the appurtenances thereof, unto the said Thomas W Glasspoole and to his heirs and assigns forever.

In testimony whereof, I, Ulysses S Grant, President of the United States of America, have caused these Letters to be made Patent, and the Seal of the General Land Office to be hereunto affixed.

Given under my hand, at the CITY OF WASHINGTON, the tenth day of May, in the year of our Lord one thousand eight hundred and Seventy, and of the INDEPENDENCE OF THE UNITED STATES the ninety fourth.

By the President: U. S. Grant
By Charles White, Sec'y.
W. _____, Recorder of the General Land Office.

RECORDED, Vol. 1 Page 492

This Homestead Grant Certificate was written for Thomas Glasspoole in section 28, town of Canton. It is dated May 10, 1870, in the 94th year of Independence of the United States. Document courtesy BCHS

squatters. Gunplay sometimes erupted. In 1841 Congress established the right of pre-emption. A person could file a land application, move onto the land and improve it (build a hut), and buy up to 160 acres for $1.25 per acre.

Homestead Act—Passed by Congress in May, 1862, the Homestead Act allowed any person over 21, who was head of a family, and who was or intended to become a citizen, to obtain title to 160 acres if he or she lived on it for 5 years and improved it. Or, the settler could purchase the land for $1.25 per acre instead of fulfilling the residency requirements. By 1891 nearly all the good farming land was settled.

Soldiers—Veterans of the Revolutionary to Mexican wars were offered land in lieu of discharge money.

Many eastern settlers followed the advice to "Go West Young Man" as soon as their soil-robbing agricultural practices depleted the land where they were. Soil depletion happened here until the settlers realized they had to get back to methods of fertilization that were practiced in Europe. Dairying became a practical way to diversify and regain the fertility of the land. Years of planting crop after crop of wheat, in addition to rust and army worms made change necessary.

The thresher replaced the reaping hook or sickle and cradle. The Meuli brothers may have been the first to use a threshing machine and supply the five or six span of horses needed to make the circuit through the neighborhood. They borrowed the machine from Sauk County and then returned it.

Kessinger observed that, "Farmers as a class are probably as intelligent as any other class of citizens, but they do not know of whom to take advice." Indeed, for a long time they preferred the advice of the reaper agent—the man with machinery to sell.

By 1910 farming claimed 91 percent of the total land area of the county. This meant more fields on steep slopes and a reduction of woodland, already depleted by lumbering. Soil erosion didn't go unheeded, but solutions took time. That same year, a pioneer conservationist, Gottlieb Muehleisen, founded the National Soil Conservation Company in Alma. He marketed erosion

These seven-hitch teams probably plowed a lot of ground in a day on the Whelan farm north of Mondovi. Photo courtesy Dell Whelan

This picture may seem out of place, but farmers also had to contend with rocks. Here a lone worker is probably thinking about what it took to put in the sewer at Alma. Photo courtesy MAHS

control devices—flumes, porous check dams, and other devices—of which some still function. Buffalo County was a leader in projects that attracted national attention as a means to save the soil. Programs that have helped:

1. County Agent since 1919 and Four-H Clubs
2. Civilian Conservation Corps program in 1930s
3. Soil Conservation Service since 1935
4. University of Wisconsin Agricultural Short Courses
5. State Plowing Contests—1951 Contest at Waumandee. Bill Moy was a state winner. Wilbert Rohrer was a state and national winner. The State Plowing Contests became Farm Progress Days.
6. State Historical Society had a traveling Cultural and Agricultural exhibit in 1984. Buffalo County had a section on Soil Conservation. Kate Stettler of Fountain City and Pauline Stamm of Modena, were coordinators.

Steam Power

When steam engines came into use, farmers knew they had it made. They loved the power and the excitement of working with the machine. Some said it could do the work of a hundred horses, but others were afraid of the danger from steam or fire. An urgent whistle signaled the need for water.

Many never got over the magic of owning or being around an engine named Advance, Case, Huber, Rumely, or countless others. Everyone learned the message of the whistle:

Morning Start-up—one long, several short blasts

Hurry Up with More Grain—three short

Lunchtime—one short

Evening Shutdown—one long that died down very low

Weather was always a factor during threshing or silo filling. The women were just as anxious to get it done as the men. Besides a big meal or two daily, the ladies prepared a mid-morning and mid-afternoon lunch. The women would try to outdo each other with the amount and variety of food. Often they served: heaping platters of roast beef, pork, or chicken; bowls of mashed potatoes and boats of gravy; stacks of fresh bread and dishes of butter, pickles, and jams and jellies of all sorts; dishes of applesauce, blueberries, strawberries, or pieplant (rhubarb); all kinds of pie—apple, mincemeat, lemon—and cakes, too; coffee cups or glasses filled continually.

This group was threshing in Bennett Valley in 1890. This type of portable steam engine was pulled by horses and was built after the late 1850s. They ranged in horsepower from eight to twenty. This rig was owned by Lewis Nyre, grandfather of Betty Norby, who lent the picture. At the top, from left to right, are Knute Nyre, unidentified, Lewis Nyre, Will Kent, Martin Norby, Ole K. Lee, Oluf Norby, and Sever Rude. In the front are Sever Lasse, Nels Sampson, Knute Larson, Martin Lee, Andrew Larson, Andrew Lee, Lewis Larson, Willie Kent, Joe Kent, Lewis Hovey, and a Larson.

This could be an early threshing machine that used a carrier to take straw away. The photograph is from the Praag area. Photo courtesy Mr. and Mrs. Wilferd Schaub

Jeremiah Gumbert is standing by the portable rig he owned prior to 1890. Straw was moved by carrier in the days before blowers were used. Photo courtesy Doris Gumbert

Jeremiah Gumbert prepares to move to the next place from Water Street, Gilmanton, in the late 1890s. The new machine was a return flue Huber, which had the stack over the firebox. It was thought to be a more efficient use of steam. The horses are ready to pull the carrier. The steam engine pulled the water wagon and thresher. Photo courtesy Doris Gumbert

This threshing crew is ready to move in the Praag area. Note that the stack is in the front of this machine. E. F. Ganz once wrote that "The machines were kept going into the winter as long as deep snow allowed for stack threshing. To lug an outfit from one valley to another on bobs was not less common than for a man to carry a borrowed breaking plow across the bluffs on his back." Photo courtesy Mr. and Mrs. Wilferd Schaub

It took a good separator man to handle the blower to make a neat straw stack. Here bundle pitchers are pitching bundles from wagons. Elmer Goss (standing on right) owned this outfit. The separator was a 32/56 Minneapolis. Claire Saxe, Sr., was driving the grain wagon with his team of Morgans—Snip and Trebly. Photo courtesy MAHS

A new steam engine was delivered to Fountain City and it had to be inspected by big and little men. Photo courtesy Armin Arms

One day a steam engine went through the board bridge at Fountain City. Photo courtesy Jim Scholmeier and Armin Arms

The Franz and Rosa Heller, Sr., home in Heller Valley, Lincoln. The Hellers had been in the county since 1866. Ready for chores are Franz, Frank, Edwin, Alfred, and Joe. Photo courtesy Mr. and Mrs. Wilfred Schaub

4

BUILDING IN THE COUNTY

Homes

Pioneers who came up the Mississippi River had to select their land and immediately build some sort of cover. Overland settlers had a wagon they could continue to live in, so a human shelter could wait a bit.

Samuel Bond described his family home as "a shanty made of tamarack poles carried from the swamp, covered with dirt and sod. Fireplace was made of large flat stones. Beds were made of poles."

Some early homes were dugouts in hillsides. A roof and sides secured it and maybe extended it a bit.

Other settlers cut logs, built huts or cabins on the level, and filled cracks with clay. They were small, often with dirt floors. Very few brought much furniture, so furnishings were made from the same rough building logs.

A bit later, they might have been able to buy some lumber to build a board shanty. As sawmills increased and money became available, nice homes were built. Stone and brick became popular materials for homes. "Homes don't make money." Women were apt to hear these words if they dared to dream about more room or some money for curtains. In the early days, they could accept that philosophy, but it didn't stop the wishful thinking.

Fritz Oppliger lived in this log home on the Andrew Ruben farm in Cross for many years. This photo taken about 1915. Photo courtesy Elmer Ruben

This log home was built on the farm Andreas Baertsch homesteaded in 1853 in Cross. This picture, taken about 1909, shows the five sons of the George and Kate Dell Baertsch family. West and Grant are seated in the cart. Standing are Oscar (back), Lee, and George. Photo courtesy Duane Baertsch

This double-wing log home of the Mattausch family was built in the Praag area. From left to right are: Gertrude Tillmann Mattausch and Augusta, Ella, Henry, Nicholas, Joseph (Sep), and William Mattausch. The Miller and Mattausch Band played in a hall located nearby and at other places. Photo courtesy MaryAnn Miller

Michael Sendelbach came to the Waumandee area in 1857. He built a "block" home about 1860 and then built this frame home in 1870. When a traveling photographer came along, the man of the house decided the barnyard "gentleman" should also be included in the picture. Photo courtesy Anton Sendelbach

This home is located on the first homestead in Yaeger Valley and was owned by a man by the name of Marolf. He lost it to the "intrigue" of the Pierce brothers. Then Robert Keith got the home and sold it to Edward Jaeger. This picture, taken in 1897, shows the brick home of the Jaegers. The bricks came from a brickyard nearby. Photo courtesy Lila Jones

Frederich Schaub came from Prussia in 1853, and was an early settler in the town of Lincoln. Frederich died when a son, William, was 19. William bought the farm from his mother, Amalia Huebsch Schaub, four years later. He married Sarah Haigh. Part of the two-family home is over one hundred years old. It is now the home of Wilfred and Catherine Molitor Schaub. Photo courtesy Mr. and Mrs. Wilfred Schaub

This home is on the National Register of Homes. It was built for Fred Laue, Jr., in 1896. It is a two-story Second-Empire home on South Main in Alma. The picture was taken about 1905 and has Charley Laue showing off his racing horses. One is Lilly Monet, filly of Dan Patch. The home is now owned by Patrick and Denise Noll, who have made it into a Bed & Breakfast. Photo courtesy Blanche Schneider

This was the farmstead of Bert and Elma Moats in the Modena area in 1911. Ira Moats homesteaded it in 1863. Photo courtesy Vera Lindsay

Farmsteads

The first barns erected by the settlers often were little more than sheds covered with wild hay to protect the oxen and chickens from the weather and wolves, or log stables built of tamarack poles, with spaces chinked with clay from the creek. As land was cleared, the settlers started putting up log barns.

When the farmers changed to dairying, there was a need for better barns. Neighbors would help each other erect barns so that work could progress quite fast. There are areas in the county where the barns all look alike if a barn builder was hired. It is interesting to note that in the biographies in the 1919 History of Buffalo and Pepin County, men got the write-up which, usually included a good description of the new barn. A few did mention the homes.

This picture of a barn raising was taken by Gesell about 1895. It was on the Peter Oesau farm in the town of Gilmanton. The barn was 50 by 120 feet. Photo courtesy Gesell Collection AHS

The view from a bluff showing the Zimmerman and Bade farms with vineyards and apple orchards about 1900. Photo courtesy Carolyn Knabe

Sure, and wouldn't a man named Lawrence Kennedy call his farm Shamrock Farm. Kennedy was born in Canada and walked to the Chippewa Valley where he worked in lumber camps. He was working in Beef Slough near Nelson in 1882 when he decided to settle in Dry Coulee. The rather unique silo on this farm was the first in the town about 1912. A gasoline engine is running the silo filler. Photo courtesy Carolyn Knabe

Filling the silo in the Alma area in 1911 with a gasoline engine used for power. Note the size of the stone silo. Photo courtesy Maassen collection BCHS

Many barns sit idle these days. At one time there were a number of round barns in the county. This one is on the Herold bluff. Photo courtesy MaryAnn Hurlburt

Early Hotels

Very early river towns needed hotels, and Alma was no exception. In 1857 a grain warehouse was built near the steamboat landing on North Main street. When the company moved, it was converted into a hotel called the Massasoit House, operating from 1866 to 1894. In its latter days, the Massasoit advertised itself as "the only $2-per-day house in the city." The hotel is next to a new structure being built as a cigar factory. This picture by Gerhard Gesell is one of his better-known ones of cattle going through town to market. Photo courtesy AHS

Farmers' Hotel was erected in 1866 by Phillip Kraft. It was purchased by John and Mary Buehler of Cochrane in 1872. They operated it as the Sherman House until 1900 when son Theodore took it over as a law office. Ted Buehler had the title of town historian. Later the building was used for the ASCS office. It is being restored. Photo courtesy Blanche Schneider

Mondovi City Hotel was built in 1878 by I. J. McDermid. When the train came to Mondovi, the hotel was remodeled, and a horse-drawn "bus" met patrons at the depot. The hotel was razed in 1906, and William Helwig built a Department Store. (Farmers Store—Bob's IGA). Photo Gallery was a busy place then. These unidentified youngsters enjoy a ride in a pony cart. Photo courtesy MAHS

The hotel at Gilmanton was built by D. C. Brown in about 1884. A story is told in the community that the Litchfields had a big family, and that Mrs. Litchfield complained about living in a too-small house. One day, Mr. Litchfield came home and tossed his wife some papers and said, "Here, old woman, is that big enough for you?" She owned the hotel! Photo courtesy Velva Molland

Recycled Buildings

If buildings became too small, they were torn down or recycled. This two-story building in Gilmanton was vacant the summer of 1858, so it became the school. About 1909 a bigger school was needed, so the top floor was moved to Water Street and put on another foundation. It was used for the Woodman Hall, later the Town Hall. The bell tower was removed. The second floor is home for a unique collection. Knowlton Peck Howard settled with the Vermonters in 1861. He enlisted in the Civil War and died in 1862. Howard's father sold his son's land for a foundation called the Howard Library Association, to be a circulating library patterned after those in Vermont. Interest from the five hundred dollars is still being used to buy new books. Membership was one dollar for life. Books were to stay within one mile of the mill, and they were kept in different places over the years.

When the new school was built, space was found for the books. Shortly before the school burned in 1952, the books had again been moved. It was an omen to the people that these books were to stay in circulation. The library is open the last Saturday of every third month. Many visited the library when the fourth Backroads Tour ended in Gilmanton in 1988. Photos courtesy Doris Gumbert and Velva Molland

Horsepower was used to move a building in Gilmanton. The structure is still used for the post office. Photo courtesy Velva Molland

In 1976 the Bear Creek Four-H Club needed a bicentennial project, so the members decided to refurbish the old Tiffany school, used as the Town Hall. They spent many hours that summer scraping, painting, and cleaning. Finished, it looked so good they announced a valley reunion, which about three hundred people attended. Many other Four-H clubs have started similar projects on schools in their neighborhoods.

The white building was the Concordia Hall, built in 1882. It was considered more of a historical and cultural building rather than an architectural delight. It was built to foster German customs and sociability. When the group disbanded, they sold to the Modern Woodmen of America. This building continued until 1955 as a center for the community. At that time, it was razed to make way for a new Catholic church. Photo courtesy Blanche Schneider

5

THEY WORSHIPED

It was a number of years before the people could build churches. In the meantime, they met in cabins or schools and eagerly awaited the infrequent visit of a clergyman.

Kessinger observed that the houses of worship accommodated the majority, but there were others who considered themselves members of no church. In the beginning, most services were in German or Norwegian. The English-speaking settlers went along with that for a time. While admitting that there may have been some tensions among these groups, as a whole there was tolerance and mutual respect for the faith of others.

Kessinger detailed the churches he had been able to document. Space doesn't allow naming them all here. Listed were seven Catholic, four German Evangelical Lutheran, four Norwegian Evangelical Lutheran, five Evangelical Reformed, three Methodist, one Congregational, one Baptist, six Evangelical Association, one Unitarian, and one nondenominational.

Many beautiful churches and/or well-kept cemeteries survive that reveal much of the history of the people of the county.

Salem Evangelical built a frame church in Montana in 1862. A brick building replaced it in 1884. This church burned in 1915 when the tower was struck by lightening. The bell fell into the flames but was saved, remolded, and put in the new church, which now is called Montana United Methodist. These men are C. W. and George Senty. Photo courtesy Hazel Amidon

Immaculate Conception in Fountain City was the first church built in the county in 1858. The frame church was replaced in 1891 with this brick and stone structure, which cost four thousand dollars. Photo courtesy Elmer Duellman

St. Michael's Evangelical Lutheran Congregation in Fountain City built their first church in 1862. This was the third church in the county. The second was the Evangelical Lutheran Church in Buffalo City. Photo courtesy FCAHS

Anders Jonsson Hove (Andrew Hovey) came to the United States in 1866. He was a peg-leg carpenter who scrambled up a ladder with the best. Anders was known as the church builder in the Dover area. He and his wife, Marta, were buried at Lookout. A marker belatedly honored the church builder. Photo courtesy Eunice Anderson

The Union Church, built by the Unitarians, was the first church in Gilmanton in 1886. The Temperance Union was connected to it. This church was free to all denominations regardless of creed or nationality, and two other groups did use it. The bell tower was struck by lightening in 1950s. In 1955 the structure was torn down, and the Lutherans built a new church. Older pictures show a shed provided for horses. Photo courtesy Velva Molland

Nelson built a two-room brick school in 1890. This pictures the lower grades and Meta Jonas, the teacher. Photo courtesy Carolyn Knabe

6

STUDYING AND LEARNING

The lack of schools was a concern of the early settlers, but they needed to take care of the bare necessities first. The first recorded school was a "private subscription" taught by Mrs. J. D. Penny of Arcadia in John Buehler's log house in 1854–1855 at Fountain City.

The first school district was organized in Belvidere at the Henry Klein home in 1855, and was taught by Fannie Bishop. John Meade taught that winter in Buffalo. In 1856 there were 102 boys and 88 girls registered in three districts.

Early schools were of logs chinked with clay; some were board shanties. Material and labor were donated. Inside, the furnishings were as primitive as the buildings—plain pine benches (often without a desk or table), a wood stove, a pail, and a dipper. The teacher also had just a bench. A homemade broom of birch twigs was in the corner. The children wrote on slates.

Later, blackboards of matched lumber painted black were added. Then desks and seats, made from green lumber, and long enough for several students, were added. These had a tendency to warp. Donated land, not usable for farming, may have been on a hillside or a soggy area, so drinking water was sometimes a problem. Schools were the very center of community life. Spelling bees, Christmas programs, end-of-the-year picnics,

The people of the area wanted their children to have a good education. In 1902 the city of Alma built a large brick Training School for seventy-five hundred dollars. It was the fourth such school in Wisconsin and was also called County Normal or County College. A graduate of Wisconsin high schools could attend tuition free. For a number of years, local youngsters attended a Model School for in-school teacher training. About 1,400 teachers graduated before the school closed in 1967. In this 1907 photograph, teachers and students took time out for a group picture. Photo courtesy Carolyn Knabe

A system of school government just sort of grew over the years. Districts had school boards, but in the early years little direction. Later, with a County Superintendent of Schools and supervising teachers, things improved—provided they were dedicated. Henry J. Niehaus was one of the dedicated and he wrote in the County School Directory in 1908:

One of the important factors in shaping the future destiny of our growing children is the teaching force in our schools. It is the mission of our Training School to prepare the teachers of our common schools for this great work so that there may be a fuller realization of the aims and purposes for which these schools are organized.

Henry Niehaus was born at Waumandee and attended schools here and in Fountain City. He taught schools in the county for several years. In 1907 he was elected County Superintendent of Schools for fourteen years. This picture of his office in the Training School should be recognized by many who have sought information on family history. This room was used by the Buffalo County Historical Society until they moved into the courthouse. Photo courtesy granddaughter, Mary Sullivan

and basket or pie socials were eagerly awaited. Religious services were also held in schools.

Language was one way the people tried to maintain their ethnic background. However, the state of Wisconsin was not favorable to the use of foreign languages in public schools. The state later modified its stance and said a second language could be taught. Some schools abused this regulation by teaching English as a course of study, but all other classes were still taught in German or Norwegian. Some private and parochial schools continued to use German or Norwegian for a long time.

The rural school that many people remember changed about 1948. One-room schools with limited facilities such as outdoor plumbing, wood heat, and sometimes only one student in a grade led to consolidation. Some schools closed, and students were bused to another larger or newer one. Opinion still varies on this move. Some feel districts lost their identity and children are on the bus too long. A large district often neglected a smaller school in order to convince that area to consolidate.

Today Buffalo County has K-12 public schools at Alma, Cochrane-Fountain City, Mondovi, and Gilmanton; parochial schools at Fountain City, Waumandee, Mondovi, and Cochrane; a number of home schools; and some students are bused elsewhere.

This school would probably be called a better-board shanty. It was the Norwegian Parochial school in Tamarack Valley (Jordet farm) north of Modena about 1912. Children may have taken time to go here only a short time each year. Photo courtesy Edith Pabst

A day off and a chance to share with our peers brought this group together for a Teacher's Convention in 1919. Photo courtesy Betty Norby

These students are all lined up and ready to welcome their families at the Christmas program at Praag School in 1910. Teacher was Sarah Loesel. Photo courtesy Mr. and Mrs. Wilferd Schaub

Recess was very important to Glenn and Alfred Mueller, Bill Weisenbeck, Christ Castleberg, and Ross Van Brunt at the Burnside school in the 1920s. Ross Van Brunt was the boy running off to try something else. Photo courtesy Ruth Van Brunt.

In 1946 Buffalo County hired Mary Ann Kinney as the first Home Demonstration Agent. Home agents wore many hats. One of the perks of the job was crowning Frank Rohrer, Cochrane, Barley King in 1947. Diane Johnson Brion became Home Extension Economist in 1976. Along with the name change came the grouping of counties; Diane allocates her time between Buffalo and Pepin counties.

A Planning meeting in the one-room Extension office in the old courthouse. John J. Zahorik (left) became the new agent in 1934. Here O. J. Sohrweide, County Superintendent of Schools, and retiring County Agent John Bollinger are helping him get started. Photo courtesy BCHS

Stone Quarries

Stone was used for buildings and bridges. When the government decided to make the Mississippi River a navigable channel in 1873, it expanded the use of a product of which Buffalo County has plenty. The Kirchner quarry north of Fountain City in one year loaded 266 barges. They used a gondola to bring rock down. The Furrer brothers had a quarry at Alma, which used four teams and thirty men to get the rock down. The Harry Brothers also had a quarry at Alma. One group used one hundred kegs of powder and two thousand pounds of dynamite to blast rock during the winter of 1913. This picture of the Oenning quarry was taken in the area of the large turn on the Fountain City Dugway in 1902. Photo courtesy Janice Kochenderfer

7

BUSINESS AND INDUSTRY

We think of Buffalo County as a farming area, but it took eleven years before the first farm was settled by Peter Schank. In reality, there has been much business and industry in the county. Not all endured, but they are a part of the county's history.

We all remember pictures of Indians smoking the peace pipe at councils of war or peace. "Tobacco taken back to Europe was converted into a luxury, in defiance of the senses." Early records show that some tobacco was grown here, but most was brought in to make cigars at Alma and Fountain City. By 1876 Alma was making over fifty thousand cigars using thirteen brand names, such as Belle of Alma and Johnnie Bird. Cigars were made until about 1920. The next group of pictures tell of some of the businesses that were engaged in throughout the county.

Lime Kilns

John Raetz burned the first lime, which sold for one dollar per barrel, at Wild's Landing near Fountain City. Julius Wilke had a kiln at Alma. This picture is of the Charles Furrer Lime Kiln at Alma. Small chunks of limestone were gathered from below the bluffs north of town (near the oil tanks) and placed on grates in the kiln's stone and brick oven. The rock was burned over a slow fire for seventy-two hours. Then it was raked out and allowed to cool. It was used as an ingredient in making mortar for masonry work. Photo courtesy Naomi Krause

This rock crusher was used at Fountain City. Photo courtesy Janice Kochenderfer

This photograph illustrates the process of making an arch stone bridge in the Praag area. Photo courtesy Mr. and Mrs. Wilferd Schaub

An elaborate double arch stone bridge in Mondovi over Peeso Creek. Photo courtesy MAHS

Flour Mills

Early settlers had to travel to Rollingstone, Minnesota, to get flour and often carried it home on their backs. The first mill was at Fountain City in 1855, built by Buehler and Clarke. Other mills were at Gilmanton, Glencoe, Mill Creek, Misha Mokwa, Modena, Mondovi, and Waumandee. This photograph show the millpond, bridge, and mill at Gilmanton. Joel Mann built the first mill in 1857 (some say 1863). Floods and wheat rust stopped flour grinding here. Around 1900, dances and other parties were held on the second floor of the mill. In 1946, Robert Hart bought the mill. He still grinds feed and has a store.

The Gilmanton millpond provided water power to run the mill, ice to supply the creamery, and skating for recreation. After the dam went out the area was an eyesore for the community until the Gilmanton Sportsman Club came to the rescue. A smaller area was banked up to form Rainbow Lake. An area was also designated a Community Park. Photo courtesy Velva Molland

The old mill and bridge over Mirror Lake in Mondovi. It was built by the Gordon brothers in 1857. A flood took the dam. Mirror Lake was cleaned up a few years ago, and the lake and park are now enjoyed by many. Photo courtesy MAHS

The Waumandee mill was built by John Oschner in 1863. His flour was the White Rose, and he also made a Wheat Gritz cereal that sold locally in many stores, and even to the Queen of England according to some. (Others report that a Fountain City flour went to Belgium.) The dam went out in a flood, so the present owner, Paul Grulka, uses the steam turbine that replaced water power to grind horse feed. Photo courtesy Gesell Collection AHS

Brickyards

The county had plenty of good clay, as evidenced by the number of brick buildings in the county. Joseph Berni had a yard in the ravine north of the Burlington Hotel in Alma in 1860. Julius Wilke built his yard in the southern section of Alma, which eventually operated five kilns from 1880 to 1902. Waumandee had two brickyards.

This scene shows the rail system for the gondolas that brought clay to the shed of the Roettiger brickyard in Fountain City. Photo courtesy Janice Kochenderfer

The H. & F. Roettiger yard in 1890. The bricks are ready to be moved to the drying shed. The crew in the front row, left to right, are Romie Heck, Bill Becker, Fred Roettiger, Louis Bruegger, Hy Roettiger, Fred Fugina, Emil Wunerlich, Hip Roettiger, and Roy or Wayne Roettiger on horse, Beauty. In the second row are Old Lang, Bill Kammueller, and Louie Hertzfeldt. At the top are Old Bone and Gink Schmidtknecht. Photo courtesy Jim Scholmeier

The drying shed for bricks at the Roettiger brickyard in Fountain City. Photo courtesy Jim Scholmeier

Sawmills

The Indians burned the bluffs for better pasture for animals, and for herbs and other food that they collected. Since this burning was usually done in the spring, the top and north sides of the bluffs were still moist so the trees were saved. Buffalo County had little hardwood at first, and the early sawmills depended on the pineries. Apparently the settlers had what they called "prairie fires" to clear land until about 1890. One of the first sawmills was that of Goehrke and Binder on Waumandee Creek. About the same time, Bishop and Carpenter built this sawmill on the lower end of Fountain City (the motel area) in 1855. The tall chimney was a landmark for many years. There were other mills at Fountain City, Alma, Buffalo City, Lower Spring Creek, and Mondovi. Photo courtesy Janice Kochenderfer

Getting up wood with lots of help on a Saturday. Photo courtesy Mr. and Mrs. Wilfred Schaub

A wood-sawing bee in the Praag area, probably at the Miller or Mattausch place. Photo courtesy MaryAnn Miller

Clarence Angst captioned this photo "cutting the dimensions for the new barn on the David Angst place." It had been the Waters farm in Upper Irish Valley. Pictured, left to right, are Henry Rotering (by the engine), Anthony Hynes, Ulrich Knecht (on the carrier), Phillip Klein and David Angst by the saw. Photo courtesy BCHS

Wineries and Breweries

A winery was one of the first industries at Waumandee. Alma, Belvidere, and Fountain City also manufactured wine. Many area pictures showed vineyards, but the climate was "too unreliable for the industry to ever amount to much."

Breweries seemed to have thrived in the lower part of the county, but Kessinger reported that "A good wee drop is appreciated by a good many in the northern part, in spite of prejudice and opposition."

The Eagle Brewery, Fountain City, built in 1857, used caves in the hillside to cool and store "Old Castle Beer." Closed during Prohibition and never reopened as a brewery, it served as an apartment building for a time. From the top: Jake Koschitz, Andrew Stettler, Jack Koschitz, Joe Beffa, Mrs. John Koschitz, Mamie Behlmer, Unidentified, Anna Koschitz, Mrs. Joe Beffa, Wilma, Elsie, and Norma Koschitz, Izetta Beffa Horstman, Roman Koschitz, and a Quinlan child. On the wagon is John Koschitz. Photo courtesy Jim Scholmeier

The Fountain Brewery about 1905—called the Yankee Brewery in lower town. It was built of local brick in 1885, when the railroad excavated land. The brewery closed during Prohibition, but reopened from the early 1930s until 1965. Its brand was Fountain Brau Beer. The building was razed for Country Apartments. Photo courtesy Janice Kochenderfer

The Malt House of Union Brewery was built in 1876. John Hemrich had a log brewery on South Main soon after 1855. In 1890, new owners changed the name to Alma Brewery. It closed in 1919. A large beer-aging cave (now sealed off) is the only evidence of this brewery. Photo courtesy Blanche Schneider

Electric Plants

Alma had an electric light plant in 1893. Gottlieb Kurtz used sixteen-candlepower lights every two blocks, plus lights in the courthouse, Commercial Hotel, and Rubens Store. About the same time, Roettigers built this plant, which operated until 1905. The men are Martin Fuerbach, Fred Roettiger, and Ambrose Herdig. Photo courtesy Janice Kochenderfer

Wind power was necessary for farmers to get water for their cattle. Many will remember days on end in the 1930s when no breeze turned the windmill. Photo courtesy Carol Knabe

The dam and spillway at Gilmanton. In 1912 a generating plant was built. On Monday two hours of washing could be done; on Tuesday two hours of ironing. On Saturday night, current was provided for a couple of hours. If there was something special happening in town, a collection of dimes was taken up to buy power. Photo courtesy Velva Molland

The Dairyland Power Plant supplies much of the area today. Coal comes in by rail and/or barge all year long.

Creameries

There had been a number of family cheese factories in Swiss settlements because that was the best way to preserve perishable milk. Almost every community had a cheese factory or creamery at some time.

Since the farmers had only a few cows, the homemaker put the milk in pans and skimmed off the cream for making butter. In time, she may have extra butter and would get regular customers to buy her product.

When the farmers owned more cows, they bought separators. Daily washing of that machine was a chore that few women learned to relish. Skim milk was a by-product of these dairies, and one inventive producer tapped into using it. When the Fountain City creamery was started, there was an island across from it where pigs and other livestock were kept. A pipe was put down to carry whey to the pigs on "Pig Island."

Skim milk was fed to pigs, and cream was taken to a local creamery or picked up by men like Charlie McCabe at the Herman Ratz farm in Eagle Valley about 1900. Note the wooden containers and the scale at the back of the wagon. *Photo courtesy Armin Arms*

The Press

The press received attention and support in the county at an early period. The Fountain City Beacon *was printed in 1856 before Winona had a paper. Its main purpose was to print the tax list in the county, and it only existed a few years. In 1861, the* Buffalo County Republikaner *at Buffalo City, and the* Buffalo County Journal *at Alma, were started in order to become the official county paper. Alma became the county seat, and also the home of the the official county paper. The people of the county also read German, Norwegian, Polish, and English newspapers.*

The Buffalo County Republikaner *was moved to Fountain City about 1864. The newspaper was printed in German until the 1920s. In 1959 it was sold to the owner of the* Cochrane Recorder, *who published the resulting newspaper until 1971, when it was sold to Valley Publisher's. Photo courtesy Jim Scholmeier*

Walter L. Houser published the Buffalo County Herald *in 1876, at Mondovi. It was "devoted to the cause of temperance, and the interests of Buffalo County." The name was changed to* Mondovi Herald-News *in 1896. Frank St. John bought the paper in 1912. Peter Peterson and Frederick Scott worked for St. John about the time this picture was taken in the 1920s. Photo courtesy MAHS*

Barbershops
At the barbershop in Fountain City a man could get a bath, shave, and haircut for fifty cents or twenty-five cents each. The barber had to clean the tub between bathers. *Photo courtesy Jim Scholmeier*

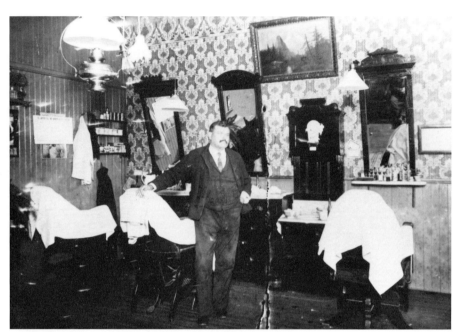

No self-respecting lady went out without her fine hat. Here is Bertha Silverness Tonner of Mondovi. Shop owners traveled to Chicago to see the latest in hats, corsets, and other finery. *Photo courtesy Eunice Anderson*

Millinery Shops
Mrs. J. B. Rothrock's Millinery Shop in 1926. Wilhelmina Grotjahn married a traveling salesman at Redwing and returned to Alma to open her shop. There were many other shops like this in the county. *Photo courtesy AHS*

Telephone
Facing page: Most areas had a telephone system of some sort in the early 1900s. This shows the Fountain City operator at work in the building that is going to be the museum of the Fountain City Area Historical Society. *Photo courtesy AHS*

Main Street, Alma, in 1917. Hardly a horse in town today. Photo courtesy AHS

8

TRANSPORTATION

The Winnebago Indian trails became the route of many roads that followed the line of least resistance along bluffs, marshes, and creeks. Kessinger said that it was thought to be more important to find a route than to worry about the grade.

David D. Davis laid out the first road in Glencoe with a uniform grade in 1870. It was called the Ridge Road. The part down to Fountain City was called a "dugway." Dugway was the word used to describe a steep, narrow, winding road needed to connect the valley to the work land on the bluff. Early settlers often dug a trail to quarry stone for their buildings. Many of these trails became town roads.

The Cincinnati Colonization Society spent money to build a road across the Belvidere bluff for the purpose of opening a market between Buffalo City and Waumandee. By 1907, counties had to outline routes of county roads.

Mr. and Mrs. Tessendorf in town with their little white oxen and fancy cart at the four corners in Mondovi. Photo courtesy MAHS

This "horseless carriage" brought the well-dressed man on business to Hudson street, Mondovi. Note the furniture store, which is still on the corner, and the entrance to the dance hall upstairs. Photo courtesy Kristi Schultz

Mondovi proclaims to be the Horse Capital of Wisconsin. In 1877 a group of Mondovi men purchased the celebrated Norman-French Percheron stallion, Horace Greeley, for two thousand dollars. He was a beautiful dapple gray, six years old, weighing fifteen hundred pounds. He was called "Old Greeley" and became the foundation draft horse of the area. Here a stallion cart is ready to make a trip to a farm. This was a familiar sight in the summer. Photo courtesy Dell Whelan

Roswell Schaub cranking up the Ford Model T. Wilma, Linda, William Schaub holding Clarence, and Mr. Machinsky are ready for a ride with Adlai Schaub. Photo courtesy Wilferd Schaub

A group in Davis Valley, Gilmanton, wonder about this new machine. Shovels were a must on trips at certain times of the year. Photo courtesy Hazel Amidon

Working the River

The Mississippi River that we see today wouldn't be recognized by the Indians, or by the traders and explorers who used it. Charles Engel didn't have a bridge to cross when he left Pepin. Present-day inhabitants in Alma recall hearing that people walked to the islands when the water was low.

Many settlers arrived by way of this river. The river has played a big part in the history of the county, but to understand a large segment of the story, two other rivers must be considered.

In 1682 the explorer La Salle wrote about the *Bon Secours* river. He had described the Chippewa River, telling how it entered the Mississippi

The office of the Mississippi Logging Company at Beef Slough. The company hired six hundred during the rafting season and kept about one hundred the rest of the year. There were several camps between Maxville and Alma for different jobs. The work was hard, wages small, and payment was not secure. A rafting job to St. Louis would take most of the summer, but there were no jobs at home. Camps had strict rules. No liquor was allowed in camp. Rivermen used to come to town with their spiked shoes that were very hard on the floor of Nogle's Hotel (Dam View), so he poured a cement floor that still exists today. Photo courtesy AHS

at the same place as the *Riviere de Beeufs* (Buffalo or Beef). *The Wisconsin Historical Collection* confirmed that story but added:

The mouth of the Chippewa River has shifted since the 17th century when it entered the Mississippi at the southern end of what is now called Beef Slough.

The route of the Chippewa River bottom lands from below Durand to Alma is shown as the Beef Slough on early maps. When the Chippewa River

Ladies Day on the river was a social event sponsored by the company. The company built a Workman's Library (also called Church on the Beef Slough) in 1884 (near Silver Moon). It was a comfortable place for men to spend time reading or writing. Any denomination was free to hold services for the men. Photo courtesy Blanch Schneider

found a new route is not known. Both areas were important for steamers going up the river and for logs coming down.

Lumbering in the Chippewa Valley began early, and this river was the route to cities on the Mississippi. The millmen of Chippewa Falls went to the state legislature to prevent others from using the Beef Slough. The Mississippi millmen organized the Beef Slough Manufacturing, Booming, Log-driving, and Transportation Company and applied for a charter, which was refused in 1867.

The Chippewa millmen sent crews to close up the entrance of the menacing slough. The Mississippi millmen protested. They prevailed upon friendly local authorities to condemn land for a public highway. Then they tore out the offending structure. Disputes and contentions continued until 1870, but by then the company was bankrupt.

In January 1871, F. Weyerhaeuser organized the Mississippi River Logging Company in Iowa. He obtained the rights to the Beef Slough Company in 1873 and the Chippewa Falls Lumber and Boom Company in 1881. This became the Chippewa Logging Company.

Logs were moved downstream by two methods—rafting and brailing. For rafting, each log was fastened in at least two places to poles by lockdowns and plugs. Poles extended across ten-foot strings. (There might be two to fourteen strings.) When brailing, the combination of logs was the same as for a raft, but the logs weren't separately connected or secured. Instead, a boom went around the entire mass. Booms were fastened by iron links and were prevented from spreading by galvanized wire at fifty-foot intervals. A brail was 550 feet long and 45 feet wide. Six brails coupled together formed a full Mississippi Raft. Each had a brail boss and a crew to land the raft. Later, steamboats were hooked to the stern. Photo courtesy Blanche Schneider

The line of pilings at the end of the peninsula (upper middle) was where logs could be held and sorted. Note the single railroad track in Alma and no buildings on that side of the road. Photo courtesy AHS

Across the river are wing dams built after 1878 to solve navigation problems. Built out from the shore to decrease the width of the channel, they let the water flow faster and carry away sand, logs, and debris. Mats of brush were made from bundles twenty feet long and fifteen inches thick. When the mat was ready and in place, the crew of the rock barge started throwing rocks onto it. This was repeated until the structure was high enough. Some are still intact. Note the opening of the cave from which this picture was taken. Photo courtesy AHS

The natural land formation of the "Bay" at Fountain City was an ideal place for a harbor and boat storage. Being midway between the Wisconsin River at Prairie du Chien and St. Paul led to the establishment of a United States Boatyard in 1889. At first the yards were on the east side of the island that separated the main channel from the city. Three barges were built and a dike was constructed. In 1894 a forty- by sixty-foot building was constructed, but in 1907 the government purchased land right in Fountain City where barges, quarterboats, and dredges were constructed. Here a crew poses at the new site. Photo courtesy Janice Kochenderfer

A view of the boatyard before World War I, taken by Hans Reuter (an unfounded rumor in the area suggested he might be a German spy). This boatyard was the home of the William A. Thompson dredge that maintained the six-foot channel from Lake Pepin to Prairie du Chien until the 1930s. Photo courtesy Janice Kochenderfer

The hydraulic dredge, Vesuvius, *was built at the boatyard in 1907. It was used to maintain the six-foot channel authorized by Congress. Photo courtesy BCHS*

President Jimmy Carter and Rosalynn took the Delta Queen *down the Mississippi on August 17, 1979. Carter was the first president to go through the locks on the river. They greeted people at Alma. Photo courtesy Larry Balk*

Getting out the ice needed for summer made good use of the river during the winter. This was done in many places in the county. Photo courtesy Blanche Schneider

Railroads

"Railroads were great developers and civilizers of our times," declared Kessinger. About half of each year, settlers had to struggle to get supplies when the river froze up. Older maps show that the government set aside land to entice railroads to build on the frontier. They could sell the land for funds.

Farmers and merchants soon realized what a benefit a railroad could be. Kessinger even accused the people in the northern part of the county of "amusing themselves with schemes and projects." As early as 1867, people everywhere were being taken in by men like a Mr. Sharpe, who "being very profuse on promises," was "very unreliable regarding performance." Many lost the hundred-dollar subscription they had paid to the promoters.

The first railroad line was one that crossed the southern tip of the county in 1870. It had been chartered to the LaCrosse, Trempealeau, and Prescott Railroad Company in 1857. It became the Chicago & Northwestern in 1867. Winona was eager to get the railroad and, therefore, had a new bridge built. The tracks were laid from LaCrosse to Winona with a station at Marshland, and later a siding at Bluff Siding. Marshland was a hub for this rail line, plus the Green Bay and Western down the east side of the Trempealeau River.

In 1882 the Milwaukee & St. Paul built a line along the Chippewa River from Eau Claire to the Mississippi below Trevino. As a result, northern farmers benefited from a closer market.

In 1882 the Chicago, Burlington & Quincy bought the right of way along the eastern side of the Mississippi to Prescott. Surveyed and plotted in 1883, the tracks were laid from Trevino to LaCrosse in 1884. Service came in 1885, and the track went further. For a long time, there was no road to Pepin, which meant that if you had business there, you drove to Durand and down the other side of the Chippewa River. Women in Nelson remember taking a train to Pepin to play basketball with the Pepin girls. Photo courtesy Carolyn Knabe

Pontoon bridge below Trevino, used to carry the train to Reads Landing. The four-hundred-foot span opened for river traffic and operated until 1951 when ice damaged it. Then it was moved to Lake City and used for a fishing pier for a time. Trevino had a depot for many years. Photo courtesy Carolyn Knabe

A closeup of the trestle. Photo courtesy Buehler Collection AHS

A view of the railroad trestle along Alma from 1885 to 1902. The trestle was over water from Tritsch's Store to Schaettles' Store (milk plant to Turtons). The river was close to buildings, and sand bars appeared in low water. In 1902 this area was filled with dredged sand and rock. Photo courtesy Gesell Collection AHS

The depot at Alma. Six passenger and ten freight trains went through daily in 1886. For a time there was also a depot at Beef Slough lumber camp. Photo courtesy Blanche Schneider

In 1924 a double track was laid from Fountain City to Alma. In 1927 it went further. Between Indian Creek Road (north of Merrick Park) and the Bechly underpass was what was called Purdy Siding. It was a switching place for trains to pass on the one-rail track. At first a couple lived in the building, but the last switcher, Robert Morning, came with a handcar from Cochrane. Photo courtesy Blanche Schneider

Dog days in Fountain City. Many people rode the "Dinky" to Winona for a day's shopping. Each day Number 52 went down and Number 54 came up. It closed in 1960. Photo courtesy Jim Scholmeier

The Mondovi Depot was located along the Buffalo River. Rail service began in June, 1890, when N. C. Foster built a track for the Chicago, St. Paul, Minneapolis & Omaha Railroad from Fairchild to Mondovi. Foster was quite proud of his railway and asked other lines to trade free passes. They declined because his line was only thirty-six miles long. He retorted, "It might be shorter but it was just as damn wide." Photo courtesy Krista Schultz

The train had to turn around at Mondovi. Photo courtesy MAHS

A group waiting for the train at Mondovi. Photo courtesy MAHS

Mondovi had a snowstorm March 15, 1917. Two days later, by evening, about two hundred volunteers had cleared ahead of the train to about eight miles from Fairchild. They walked into town but found everything closed. The hotel and cafe opened to feed and house them. The next day the snowplow came, and they returned to Mondovi. They received expenses but no pay. Photo courtesy MAHS

Fountain City

It was here that the settlement and political organization of the county began in 1839, with the arrival of the Holmes party. Some have said that the name Holmes Landing was more picturesque and easier to explain. But Holmes didn't stay very long, so it became the Indian Wah-mah-dee. When the people couldn't get used to the name, it was changed to Fountain City in 1852 because "among the many springs one had become a fountain." The village was laid out in 1855, and it was incorporated in 1870. There is a German flavor to the city. This picture, taken before 1867, shows log homes and a vineyard. The second home on the bottom was the Baertsch home. The brick building in the center is now the home of the Fountain City Historical Society. Photo courtesy Duane Baertsch

9

CITIES AND SETTLEMENTS

The northern part of Fountain City was called Germania for the many German settlers. The southern part was called Yankee Town. These winter hills must have been photographed after 1886 because the railroad was here. Photo courtesy Janice Kochenderfer

The summer hills at Fountain City were perhaps photographed a few years later. The hills were called the goat pasture. Photo courtesy FCAHS

Marshland

Marshland Station, or Marshland, was an important hub for two railroad lines across the southern tip of the county. There was a post office at the depot. There are only a few homes here now, but the Hillside Fish House had an interesting history in another era. During the thirteen years that the Volstead Act was in force, the Marshland Hotel was busy supplying bootleggers. Nearby stills and breweries provided home-brew beer, moon whiskey, and wildcat beer—all of which were sold by the owner of the hotel. Stories claimed that much of these spirits went to Chicago. Now the Hillside Fish House is an enjoyable place to dine. Near Marshland was a place called Atlanta Station on early maps, now called Bluff Siding. It was formerly the site of an extensive lime-burning industry. A railroad siding was used to load the lime.

91

This 1908 photo shows the Flat Iron Building wedged between Main and South Shore Drive, which has been a landmark. It was built in the 1860s and is used for apartments now. There is still a fountain in the tip of the intersection to commemorate the one that was sold for scrap in World War II. Photo courtesy Jim Scholmeier

Fountain City was a farmers' town. Photo courtesy Jim Scholmeier

These farmers had just taken delivery of new wagons from C. F. Prussing & Co. A stop at the Golden Frog finalized the transaction. Vom Golden Frosch *was built in 1878 by William Kruer. It had a large tin replica of a frog over the entrance. It was the favorite stopping place for loggers, and later, men working on the dam. Farmers driving cattle down from the ridge for shipment by boat cashed their checks at the Golden Frog. One owner even set up a teller's cage inside the door for this purpose. Rumor has it that the Golden Frog may reopen soon. Photo courtesy Armin Arms*

The Schultz Bakery and Ice Cream Parlor in 1897. The house built in 1856 had been used as a bakery. Later it became a cafe and also sold some groceries. Photo courtesy Jim Scholmeier

City of Buffalo

Buffalo City is the only "chartered and nonexistent" city in the county, and also the smallest city in the state. The Colonization Society of Cincinnati, "imagining that this place offered facilities and guarantees for a thriving and permanent business" purchased the land in 1855. The financial backers had great expectations, absentee owners paid their taxes, but only at high tide could boats land here. The city was chartered in 1855. Buffalo City is the third largest community in the county with a population of 918.

Three miles north of the city there was a settlement on Pomme de Terre Slough settled by Nicholas Liesch in 1848. In 1856 it was called "Village of Belvidere," but in 1858 "City of Belvidere." Pomme de Terre roughly means "land of potatoes," which were grown by John Peter Stein. Indian women used to dig them, and each night they took potatoes home for their pay. It was said that the Indian men stood around grunting their approval. To Stein also goes credit for growing the first wheat and barley in the county. Buffalo City is, in many respects, a retirement city that stretches along the river. This is a view approaching the area.

Alma

Three bachelors settled near Twelve Mile Bluff in 1848. About 1850 the name was changed to the short name Alma at the suggestion of W. H. Gates. The village was surveyed and plotted in 1855, but remained a part of the Town of Alma until 1868. It became a city in 1885. The city has a Swiss look. The population is now 848. Carriages still lined Main Street in the early 1900s.
Photo courtesy Blanche Schneider

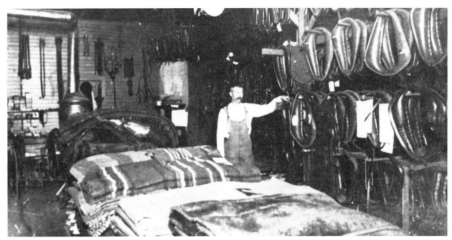

The Willie Duerkop Harness Shop in 1911. The business had previously been a shoe and boot shop. Alma also had a wagon factory from 1865, which made forty wagons a year besides carriages, sleighs, and cutters. (Tenney Telephone.) Photo courtesy AHS

Noll's General Store had a demonstration of Majestic ranges in 1917. Gladys Fetting was the little girl in the light coat in front. She remembers that they got candy for posing. Photo courtesy AHS

The playground on Second Street. Photo courtesy Blanche Schneider

Mondovi

Ole Nyseth had a woodworking shop that he sold to Mondovi for its City Building. It housed the fire department, which was organized in 1894 with forty-two volunteers. They had one hose and one ladder wagon. The first teamster to get to the station pulled the hose wagon and got five dollars. The other teamster got three dollars. Photo courtesy MAHS

An alternate way to Second street—about fifty steps. Photo courtesy Blanche Schneider

Fourteen corn binders were delivered to Mondovi area farmers August 29, 1910, by Armour and Hovey Implement Company. Photo courtesy MAHS

Barstow Bakery and Soda Fountain. Jack Gavin is behind the counter. (C to C.) Photo courtesy MAHS

Putzier Corner. Gus Putzier bought an old frame building that included a restaurant in 1903. He built this brick building in 1908. Photo courtesy Leo Smith Collection MAHS

Gilmanton
The Ferry brothers settled here in 1856. In 1857, Joel Mann started a mill on the creek, and the village went by the name of Mann's Mill. However, from 1858 to 1895 there was a post office called Gilmantown on records of the Wisconsin Postal Society. From 1895, records list it as Gilmanton. Gilmans were early settlers in the town. A fisherman tries his luck from the bridge near the dam. Photo courtesy Edna Bjorgo

Main Street before 1910. Gilmanton was a busy hub. The village had a mill, mail from two directions, stores, hotels for stagecoaches, and a library. But the railroad went to Mondovi. Photo courtesy Doris Gumbert

The middle building was the Kenyon Store/Hall, which also had the post office. It is gone, but a small building was moved in to be the post office. The bank and the third building survive. Photo courtesy Velva Molland

Dover Street going toward Lookout (Highway 121). Across from the homes is the Gilmanton High School. In 1947, community-minded citizens rallied to promote a Community Fair, which now takes place each July. Photo courtesy Edna Bjorgo

Lookout

Lookout was an active center along the stagecoach route from Independence. There was a general store, cheese factory, a school, and a Norwegian Lutheran Church. The name goes back to the Indians who used the bluff nearby as a lookout post, and because Chauncey Cooke likened it to Lookout Mountain, which he had seen during the Civil War. In 1990, Loren Nelson petitioned the state to have an "unincorporated" sign returned to Lookout.

Nelson
Coming from Alma, the DeGroff building greets us. It was used for the post office (now Laundromat). Many area buildings had the same design. Photo courtesy Carolyn Knabe

Mamre Hurlburt had a Flour & Feed, Hay & Straw Store. Photo courtesy MaryAnn Hurlburt

Walkers Department Store at Waumandee. They also sold farm supplies if you note the sign for La Crosse Plow Co. Later this store was called Cranberry's Store. Photo courtesy Hazel Amidon

Waumandee

Waumandee is in the heart of the fifteen-mile-long Garden Valley near Waumandee Creek and surrounded by bluffs to the north and south. Conrad Oschner owned much of the land when the village was plotted in 1871. Before Caspar Schmitz opened a store here in 1862, the people had to travel to Alma, Buffalo City, or Fountain City for supplies. By 1867, the German Catholics had a church and later a school that could board students. Johann Ganz and others built a two-story school modeled after the schools of his native Switzerland. It provided living quarters for the teacher, which assured good teachers. Very early there was a stagecoach stop here, so a hotel, stores, blacksmith shops, shoe repair shops, and saloons were also listed for the village. Of special note is the bank built in 1914. It survived the bank holiday in 1933—closed only ten days at no loss to depositors. It lost some cash in a burglary later, but the safe couldn't be opened. The Waumandee Bank, through its directors, officers, and employees is supporting the publication of this history.

Cream

This settlement was called Eagle Creek at first, although it was on Little Waumandee Creek. The name Cream may have come from the creamery that was here. It also had a general store, a saloon, a school, and a church. The first county fairs were held near this field from 1872 to 1876. A story told is that the fair was moved because there was only one drinking and eating spot. It first went to Alma, but flooding caused it to move to Mondovi. *Photo courtesy Armin Arms*

Cochrane

At first it was called St. Petersburgh in honor of Peter Schugg, considered the founder of the village. When the railroad was coming through in 1884, the people of Buffalo City were concerned that their cows would be killed on the tracks, so the line was moved east about two miles. The railroad secured land in the area and sold it to the St. Paul Land Company, which plotted and sold lots in 1886. When the depot was built, the railroad people called it Cochrane. This bird's-eye view of Cochrane from the bluff must be before 1924, because there is only one railroad track. *Photo courtesy Gary Schlosstein*

Small Community Settlements

There were small community centers at different places in the county.

Cross was later called Bohri, because of the settlement of Christian Bohri and four sons. There was a post office here and a community hall.

Glencoe had a church and cemetery, but today only the well-kept St. Joseph's Cemetery marks the spot.

Herold was a small community center on Highway E from Alma. William Herold was here in the early 1860s. The center had a general store, a school, a blacksmith shop, and a church.

Praag, along Highway 88, was named by William Mattausch, for his native Prague in 1852.

Montana was a neighborhood community on county U where a church has been since 1862. One day the Historical Society got a letter from South Dakota seeking help on a family genealogy. The reason they turned to us was because in an estate they found a card from Montana, Wisconsin.

Misha Mokwa was a bustling community along the Beef Slough (Highway 25) of over four hundred, around 1870, because of the logging enterprises. The name means "Strong Indian" (some say "Little Bear"). It was plotted by Mrs. Mary Prindle in 1878 and had five streets. The government built a wing dam in 1889 that caused the slough to silt up, and this was the beginning of the end of the village.

Mayville Station was never much more than a depot for the trains going down the Chippewa River below Maxville Prairie. Boats were able to come into the area also.

Modena was ". . . another little village, not of course incorporated, nor regularly laid out, containing stores, a schoolhouse, two blacksmith shops, the mill and also the postoffice." In the 1860s, the village was part of the underground railroad that helped slaves fleeing the South on the way to Canada. One died and was buried here. There is a Modena, Italy, also.

Maxville was an unincorporated community on Maxville Prairie, settled about 1858. The name honors a merchant who arrived with supplies needed by the settlers.

Urne was settled by Ole J. Urne and he was the postmaster of Urnes Corner in 1872, started for the "accommodation of the people in the upper valleys of Little Bear Creek." There is still a small community at Urne.

Tell

On a corner on Highway 37 north of Alma is a settlement called Tell, named by the early Swiss settlers for their legendary hero, William Tell. Records go back to 1866, when a hotel and store were built. The present store was built in 1903 to house the men working the woods. Later, it was used for dances, plays, and socials. Now it is operated as the Tell Store and Tavern by Junior Reidt. The pond nearby features car races on the ice each winter.

10

THEY PLAYED
THEY CELEBRATED

Excursions on the Mississippi were a regular event. Here, on a Sunday afternoon, thirty-five from Nelson embarked for a ride on the river. Photo courtesy Carolyn Knabe

Young and old enjoying an afternoon skating on the Mississippi River with Alma in the background. Photo courtesy Blanche Schneider; from the Louise Radke Collection

Gilmanton Dramatic Club about 1910. In the back row, left to right, are Linda Clark, Wayne LaDuke, Tom Litchfield, Carrie Baker, Clarence Rud, Cloe Clark, and Charles Clark. In the front row are Earl Britton, Olive Turner, Sever Severson, Edna Clark, and Sue Gumbert. Photo courtesy Doris Gumbert

An outing of the Plett and Mattausch families and some friends on the Alma Bluff (Buena Vista Park). Standing in the back row, left to right, are Joe Plett; Willie Mattausch; Rinhold, George, Helen, Gustave, and Selma Plett; Henry Mattausch; Clara Plett; and Augusta Mattausch. In front are Frank Dowiasch; Enid Hammer; Tillie, Emelia (Mrs Henry), and Joseph Mattausch; and Adolph Plett. Photo courtesy MaryAnn Miller

Most areas had their own ball teams. Judge G. L. Pattison (left front) played with the Bear Creek team in the early 1900s. Photo courtesy Jim Pattison

Looks like Isabelle Fedie (Wittig) needs help pulling Margaret and Albert. The yard had all the modern conveniences—clothes dryer, woodpile, and outhouse. Photo courtesy MaryAnn Hurlburt

Not knowing the story of this picture, all that can be said is that it looks like a bit of horseplay. John Luetcher was the "horse" and Bert Brown the driver. One Price Cash Store was in Mondovi. Photo courtesy MAHS

This is a family celebration with patriarch John Niehaus and his family. In the upper right corner are his children—Henry J., Minnie, and Louise. John had come to America in 1842 and fought in the Mexican War. He returned to Germany, married, and had five children by the time he returned to Waumandee in 1870. A son, Henry, was born here and became a teacher in our schools. Photo courtesy granddaughter Mary Sullivan

The barn was raised, so these neighbors lifted a cup to celebrate on the Fitchenbauer farm in 1917. The log barn behind the men is still on the farm. Photo courtesy Fitchenbauer family

When people heard the news that the armistice had been signed, they came out to celebrate in Fountain City on November 11, 1918. One man came in such a hurry that his flag was upside down. Fifteen Fountain City men died in the war. Photo courtesy Jim Scholmeier

"Hey, did I miss the Fourth of July parade?" Photo courtesy Jim Scholmeier

One bit of history that should not be forgotten is the place of the bench that was part of the scenery. Here one could swap stories, wait for a spouse, or discuss events of the day. Norwegians had a term for it—Sladder Borg—the name for a general store, because it was the center of gossip. Another common gathering place was at the creamery when farmers took their cream in. These benches were in front of Fred Benkert's General Merchandise Store in Nelson. Photo courtesy Carolyn Knabe

11

POTPOURRI

Great River Road

The unique geography of Buffalo County meant many former Indian trails became roads that are followed on our Backroad Tours. The settlers often gave them names whose origins are forgotten but remain colorful. People enjoy finding Pretzel Pass, Sauerkraut Crossing, or Grasshopper Ridge on a rustic fall drive.

Wisconsin tourism actively promotes another route in the county. Early photos called it Trail 35—now designated part of the Wisconsin Great River Road, which follows the Mississippi. A brochure has been published, but unfortunately a picture of the Minnesota route was used.

Work was started on our part of the road in 1952, from Winona to Fountain City. About 1985, plans were made to go further, and after much planning only five homes on the north end of Fountain City had to be removed.

This early photo of Trail 35 is between Cochrane and Alma by the Brinkman Farm. "It was a dustbowl in summer, a quagmire when it rained and was miserable in the winter." Photo courtesy Blanche Schneider

This air photo scene, taken by Carol Knabe in 1990, is a bit closer to Alma. It shows the Twelve Mile Bluff and the even taller smokestacks of the Dairyland Power Plant.

Coming from Highway 37 you can take the Great River Road either way. It also goes by Highway 35.

This photograph shows the road between Alma and Nelson as it was at one time. Photo courtesy Blanche Schneider

The road going north out of Nelson in 1908. Photo courtesy Carolyn Knabe

Landmarks
Indian Head Sentinel on the Mississippi is called the most natural stone face known. It measures forty-four feet from chin to forehead. Note the man below it for comparison. As you ride north toward Fountain City you need to watch carefully, for you can spot it only briefly. If you are coming from Fountain City you might see the Three Sisters bluffs in the same area. Since these two landmarks are on our scenic Great River Road, it seems a shame that there is not a signpost announcing them. This postcard called it Trail 35. Photo courtesy Armin Arms

Eagle Bluff, at 1,151 feet, as seen from lower Fountain City, is the highest point along the Mississippi. Photo courtesy Armin Arms

Twelve Mile Bluff was given this name long before the first settlers came in 1848. It was named by the river pilots for a prominent rock formation on the bluff (above the cemetery), because they could see it from the mouth of the Chippewa River. On moonlit nights it was a good guide. Photo courtesy Blanche Schneider

For years people watched the rock known as Pinnacle Rock, which was situated on Twelve Mile Bluff. It was of such size and altitude that they always knew someday it could come crashing down. Its height was estimated at from seventy-five to two hundred feet and it was about thirty feet around. In April, 1881, an earthquake sound was heard and the bluff seemed to move. The rock had plowed the side of the bluff for three hundred feet. Three pieces were the size of small homes. It stopped short of the sawmill but wiped out the shooting range. Photo courtesy Dell Whelan

Twin Bluffs overlooking the lower end of Nelson along Great River Road. Photo courtesy Carolyn Knabe

Beef Slough has the only historical marker presently in the county. It is along the Great River Road north of Alma and tells the history of lumbering in the Beef Slough.

APPENDIX A
Buffalo County Schools—1932

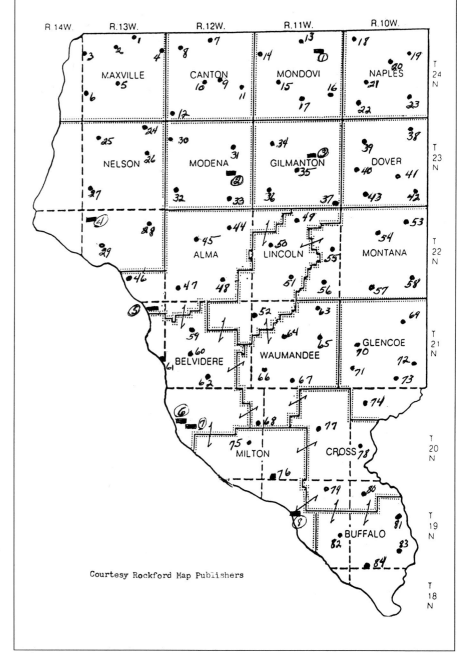

Courtesy Rockford Map Publishers

1. Oak Hill
2. Spring Creek
3. Lower Spring Creek
4. Maxville Bluff
5. Traun Bluff
6. Maxville Prairie
7. Walkers Corner
8. Newton
9. Heck Valley
10. Tiffany
11. Kelly Valley
12. North Branch
13. Harvey
14. Mondovi-Canton
15. Thompson Valley
16. Waste Valley
17. Devaney
18. Bond-Peeso
19. Hillard
20. Pace-Naples
21. Seyforth
22. Armour Valley
23. Norden
24. Burnside
25. Cascade
26. Norwegian Valley
27. Dry Coulee
28. Trout Creek
29. Deer Creek
30. Church Valley-Urne
31. Sisson
32. Pine Creek Bluff
33. Rockwell
34. Gilman Valley
35. Oak Grove
36. Griffin
37. Four Corners
38. Meadowbrook
39. Lower Bennett Valley
40. Threemile Creek
41. Lookout
42. Rindahl
43. Davis
44. Island-Hutchinson
45. Tell
46. Iron Creek
47. Mill Creek
48. Alma Ridge
49. Whelan-Lincoln
50. Praag
51. Jahn's Valley
52. Cream
53. Upper Montana Ridge
54. Buell Valley
55. Sharp Corner
56. Hanson
57. Hillside
58. Montana Ridge
59. Herold
60. Little Bluebell
61. Lakeview
62. Rose Valley
63. Lincoln
64. Garden Valley
65. Irish Valley
66. Anchorage
67. Schoeppes Valley
68. Oak Valley
69. Pecks
70. Upper Irish Valley
71. Upper Eagle Creek
72. McWeeney
73. Cowie
74. Oak Grove
75. Garden Valley Entrance
76. Fairview
77. Eagle Valley
78. Doelle
79. Cross
80. Bohris Valley
81. Platt
82. Buffalo Ridge
83. Marshland
84. Bluff Siding

City Schools
1 Mondovi
2 Modena
3. Gilmanton
4 Nelson
5 Alma
6 Buffalo City
7 Cochrane
8 Fountain City

APPENDIX B
U.S. Post Offices

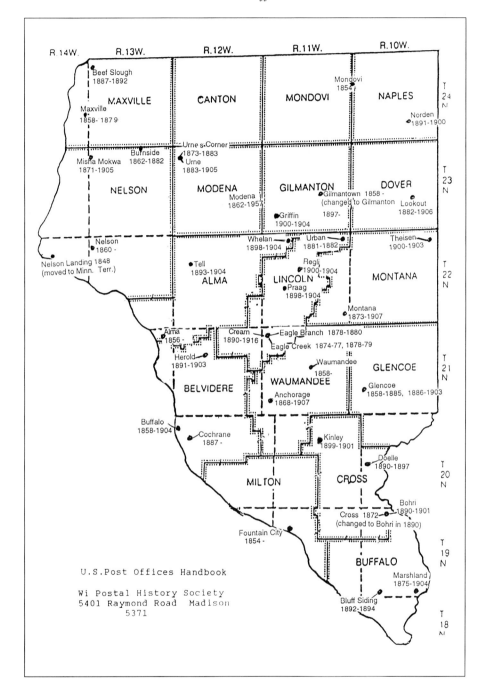

BIBLIOGRAPHY

General References

Atlas and Farm Directory with Complete Survey in Township Plats of Buffalo County, Wisconsin. St. Paul, Mn.: The Farmer, Webb Publishing, 1914.

Illustrated Historical Atlas of the Counties of Buffalo and Pepin, Wisconsin. Pardeeville, Wi.: Briggs and Falconer, 1878.

Standard Atlas of Buffalo and Pepin Counties, Wisconsin. Chicago: George A. Ogle and Company, 1896.

Books

Amidon, Hazel. *Histories of Gilmanton and Dover Townships,* 1982.

Anderson-Sannes, Barbara. *Alma on the Mississippi.* Alma, Wi.: The Alma Historical Society, 1980.

Andreas, A. T., Publisher. *History of Northern Wisconsin.* Chicago: The Western History Company, 1881.

Forrester, George, ed. *Historical and Biographical Album of the Chippewa Valley.* Chicago: A. Warner, 1892.

Franklyn Curtiss-Wedge, comp. *History of Buffalo and Pepin Counties, Wisconsin.* Winona, Mn.: H. C. Cooper and Company, 1919.

Fugina, Jeanne, and Duane Baertsch, comps. *Geschichte Von Fountain City, Wisconsin 1839–1939 (Stories of Fountain City, Wisconsin).* 1989.

Kessinger, Lawrence. *History of Buffalo County, Wisconsin.* Alma, Buffalo County, Wi., 1888.

Rockwell, Houser F. *West Central Wisconsin and Mondovi Area History.* Mondovi, Wi.: University of Wisconsin-Eau Claire-University Copy Corner, 1988.

Articles

Ganz, E. F. "Early Education in Buffalo County, Wisconsin." St. Paul, Mn.: The Twin City Buffalo County Association, 1934.

Ganz, E. F. "Lawrence Kessinger, Buffalo County Historian."

Hess, Albert. "Saint Petersburgh-Cochrane." Newspaper article, 1963.

Knowles, L. P.: Secretary and Historian of Twin City Buffalo County Association. Newspaper articles on "Mondovi History, The First Twenty Years." 1930–1940s.

Niehaus, Henry J. "Education in Buffalo County." Article in the 1919 *History of Buffalo and Pepin Counties, Wisconsin.*

Origin and Legislative History of County Boundaries in Wisconsin. Madison, Wi.: The Wisconsin Historical Records Survey. Works Projects Administration (WPA), 1942.

U. S. Post Offices Handbook. "Post Offices in Buffalo County Wisconsin." Wisconsin Postal History Society, Madison, Wisconsin.

Newspapers

Cochrane Recorder
Buffalo County Journal
Mondovi Herald News
Winona Sunday News

ABOUT THE AUTHOR

Mary Ann Pattison has been recognized by the Wisconsin Historical Society for her on-going support in the highly acclaimed Buffalo County Historical Society Backroads Tours. It was during her term as interim director of the County Historical Society that plans for the county road tour began. Mary Ann has since written seven of the eight tour guides and is involved annually in planning the tours.

Mary Ann describes herself as a "stickler for history," and in her quest for it she has coauthored a church history and a family history, and she has written two family histories.

Mary Ann was the first home agent at the University of Wisconsin Extension office in Buffalo County. She and her husband, Jim, have eight children. Through her work and her family, she has come to know well the county, its people, and of course, its history.